"Andy's biblical gift descriptions and model are foundational to solid identity and the joy that comes in walking in what you were made for. It is clear that his goal is not about the gifts but about the Giver—the 'one thing' of being led by the Spirit in connection with God. I know his blueprint will provide direction for many searching for their purpose and identity."

Jennifer Barnett, executive director, Freedom Prayer;
author, *First Freedoms*

"Andy's revelation regarding spiritual gifts is only surpassed by his heart for the Body of Christ to be equipped to function in their gifting. I highly recommend this book and its insight for every follower of Jesus—seasoned saint and new convert alike!"

Pastor Steve Berger, founder and president,
Ambassador Services International

"Finally some clarity! As the pastor of a large nondenominational church, it has been a struggle to unify the cornucopia of perspectives about spiritual gifts. Reese brilliantly honors varied traditions while inviting everyone to the table. Solid theology partnered with principles that are refreshingly applicable make this book a must-have."

Brad Bowen, lead pastor, Heritage Church

"If you are a newcomer to the area of the Holy Spirit and want some insight that will help you gain traction with this Divine Helper, this book is for you. If you have been a believer for years, but still feel that you could use some help in understanding how the Holy Spirit works in His various ways, and how the various listings of Holy Spirit work flow together, this book is for you. I can almost guarantee you will profit from listening to Andy. I gladly recommend this book."

Dr. Don Finto, pastor; founder, Caleb Company;
author, *Your People Shall Be My People*

"*The Spiritual Gifts Blueprint* is a wonderful prequel to Andy Reese's outstanding work *Freedom Tools*. In this new book, Andy Reese has created a primer on the understanding and practice of spiritual gifts. In essence, it is a master class on the subject—profitable for teaching, reproof, correction, and training in righteousness, that the man of God may be complete, equipped for every good work."

Dr. David Kyle Foster, Mastering Life Ministries

"Understanding the role and power of the Spirit is a lifelong pursuit of the head and the heart. While there are no experts on the Trinity, there are helpful guides who walk alongside us as we navigate our role in God's big story. Andy has proven to be a helpful teacher and writer, and I know this book will give you insight in your pursuits of the Kingdom being made manifest in everyday life!"

Dr. Josh Graves, lead minister, Otter Creek Church;
author, The Simple Secret

"In *The Spiritual Gifts Blueprint,* author Andy Reese has once again produced a treasure. Yes, Christians have different perspectives on gifts, but Andy clearly describes the relevant Scriptures, especially Romans 12. As a rainbow gives hope, the gifts are diffused in this prism into seven primary colors. There is one Lord, the Light, but here the many colored gifts of the Spirit lead us back to Him."

Stephen Mory, MD, DLH, psychiatrist

"Spiritual transformation must always be grounded in biblical and practical teaching. In this book the author shares a systematic process of maturing into the person God created us to be and allows one to identify spiritual giftedness. This discovery gives way for each one to become a person of purpose and to begin to experience the smile of God."

Rhonda Lowry, retired assistant professor of spiritual formation,
Lipscomb University; spiritual mentor

"As a Vineyard pastor for the past thirty years, and a third-generation pastor kid from the Pentecostal and charismatic traditions, I thoroughly enjoyed the 'good professor' Andy's wonderful explanation and encounter of the use of spiritual gifts, and how they are displayed in his writing—the pastor/teacher gifts working hand in hand to lead us to a greater understanding of spiritual gifts. I highly recommend it!"

Jon Sterns, pastor, Franklin Vineyard Church; former regional
leader, Southeast Vineyard Churches

"*The Spiritual Gifts Blueprint* is a fresh and essential tool that untangles, declutters, organizes, and simplifies what has often been made overly complex. With a laser focus on Scripture, Andy shows us how to connect to the holy Trinity to receive and use what he beautifully describes as our 'grace package.' In doing so, he leads us to discover and dive into layer upon layer of depth within the things of the Spirit."

Rob Touchstone, director, Center for Vocational Discovery,
and instructor, College of Business and College of Bible
and Ministry, Lipscomb University

THE
SPIRITUAL
GIFTS
BLUEPRINT

THE
SPIRITUAL
GIFTS
BLUEPRINT

GOD'S DESIGN FOR YOUR GIFTS,
TALENTS, AND PURPOSE

ANDY REESE

Chosen

a division of Baker Publishing Group
Minneapolis, Minnesota

© 2023 by Andrew J. Reese

Published by Chosen Books
Minneapolis, Minnesota
www.chosenbooks.com

Chosen Books is a division of
Baker Publishing Group, Grand Rapids, Michigan

Library of Congress Cataloging-in-Publication Data
Names: Reese, Andrew J., author.
Title: The spiritual gifts blueprint : God's design for your gifts, talents, and
    purpose / Andy Reese.
Description: Minneapolis, Minnesota : Chosen, a division of Baker Publishing
    Group, [2023] | Includes bibliographical references.
Identifiers: LCCN 2023010177 | ISBN 9780800763251 (trade paper) | ISBN
    9780800729998 (casebound) | ISBN 9781493441075 (ebook)
Subjects: LCSH: Gifts, Spiritual—Biblical teaching. | Christian life. | Bible.
    Epistles of Paul—Criticism, interpretation, etc.
Classification: LCC BT767.3 .R44 2023 | DDC 234/.13—dc23/eng/20230530
LC record available at https://lccn.loc.gov/2023010177

Author is represented by Ambassador Literary Agency, Nashville, TN

Baker Publishing Group publications use paper produced from sustainable for-estry practices and post-consumer waste whenever possible.

23   24   25   26   27   28   29   7   6   5   4   3   2   1

To my wife, Susan, four children,
mates, and grandchildren.
I am so very blessed by this gifted,
joyful, and all-in family.

Contents

Foreword

This is Dr. James W. Goll, the founder of God Encounters Ministries and GOLL Ideation LLC, an author or co-author of more than forty books, a certified Life Languages coach, a recording artist, a founding member of the Apostolic Council of Prophetic Elders and Harvest International Ministries, a father to four, and a grandfather to eleven at this point and time. But why did I awkwardly open up a foreword to a book like that? Well, among the many hats I have worn in my life, my family has also been a neighbor to some incredibly dear people. It brings tears to my eyes and joy to my heart to remember the sweet times when some of the Reese kids came and hung out with the Goll clan. And now our brilliant prodigies from both families are all grown-up, married, walking out their life choices, and making their marks in life.

Yes, I personally know the author of this book, Andy Reese. I have had the distinct privilege and benefit of knowing Andy in multiple settings over the past 25-plus years. He has been one of the nation's top engineers by trade; the founder of Freedom Prayer; a stargazer by hobby; an instructor, teacher, and educator at heart; and a disciple of the Lord Jesus Christ. His passion is to see people know their true identity in Christ and discover their destiny in Him. This quest has now led him to author *The Spiritual Gifts Blueprint*.

Andy and I hold many things in common. We both love the Word of God, and we both glean from various streams in the Body of Christ, historically and in the present day. In my book *Releasing Spiritual Gifts Today*, I wrote,

> My three main purposes for this book are *information*, *inspiration*, and *impartation*. First, that the information presented here will bring you into a greater awareness of biblical truth about spiritual gifts. Second, that you will be inspired, through the personal and biblical stories, to greater levels of hope and faith regarding the tremendous potential of the gifts God has given to you. Third, that you will be imparted by the Spirit with the courage to step forward and use them.

After reviewing this manuscript, I believe that once again my friend Andy and I have found yet another place of common ground. Remember, it's a three-cord strand that will not quickly be torn asunder! I believe this book is also filled with those same three ingredients—information, inspiration, and impartation.

So it's my deep honor and wonderful privilege to commend to you a book that I do not have the skill set or the technical capacity to orchestrate and compose. But thank the Lord, I have a friend and fellow member in the Body of Christ who does! Thank you, Andy, for building bridges and aiding people to safely walk into the beautiful land where gifts are freely given and fruit is maturely grown for the glory of God!

Your fellow servant,
James W. Goll

Acknowledgments

To my extended Freedom Prayer team, you are my inspiration as you labor quietly in many countries to teach us that "it was for freedom that Christ set us free." You also help us find that precious freedom, and then help us all say, "I am free unto . . . this!"

To Brad, Rob, Jen, Mike, Jeannie, Hugh, Ghislain, Loral, the HeartPrint writers' group, and many others who provided improvements to both my engineering of English and my ideas, you have provided moral support over the years of this book's development and testing.

Preface

Thank you for reading this preface. You are among the few and the brave. I'll make it worth your while.

For about 45 years, every once in a while in a large variety of settings, someone has asked me something like, "Do you know what your spiritual gift is? If so, how did you figure it out!?" Early on I never had a good answer for that question. And I was not sure it was even worth the trouble. Most in my circles had long ago settled on the idea that it is unknowable and probably not worth knowing. More on that in chapter 1.

Yet in our Freedom Prayer ministry, thousands of individuals have been freed from constraints targeting their calling and purpose. And they ask themselves the obvious question, "What am I freed *to*?" They deserve an answer. This book is designed to answer that question.

Even yesterday, I was with a young woman who was stuck in a frustrating controversy, and she was sent to me by her counselor to help her figure it out. In maybe thirty minutes, we walked through who she really was; we talked about what truly motivated her and how it did, what seemed to link the best steps in her life, and what her sense was of the smile of God the Father. Somewhere near the end of our time she exclaimed, "That explains it! Thank you so, so much."

Jesus demonstrated a high regard for Scripture, often confounding the scribes and Pharisees with His "Have you not read?" statements.* Over the decades of Scripture study, project development, and practical application, I have developed a similar regard.† And the patterns and truth that can be uncovered on this book's topic are sort of mind blowing to me.

This book is designed to do for you what the thirty-minute discussion with the young woman did for her. It is designed to intrigue and stir up amazement at the patterns of purpose-producing truth hidden in plain sight for us to find, as it has done for me over the years. It is presented to be an easy and helpful read.

I want you to know that I fully understand, maybe more than most, that this topic has been taught thousands of times and written about tens of times, and that there are many mutually exclusive definitions of the term *spiritual gifts*. And I deeply respect and have learned from each one of those books. I've put this book off for over a decade for just those reasons—but no longer.

This book might be seen as a bit of a departure from some of the standard approaches, even radical. But then, so was Paul's response to the confused Corinthians in 1 Corinthians 12. And I tried to follow his corrective explanations laid out in several places in Scripture point by point. You will see that Paul's response goes far, far beyond "spiritual gifts" and outlines a comprehensive approach to Christian life itself that has proven to be biblical, practical, God-connecting, and transformative.

As such, this book is designed for a pastor, professor, or Bible study leader to be satisfied that the book is not simply yet another set of an author's good ideas—not just popular literature. It is designed to be faithful to scriptural exegesis and to the original meanings of texts and their variants. It is designed, along with the workbook, for Bible studies, college classes, and sermons. It can, however, be a bit dense in places. It is designed to change you if you let it. It is designed to last.

---

*For example, Matthew 12:3, 5; 19:4; 21:16, 42; 22:31

†See, for example, "The Magi Project," YouTube.com, September 20, 2013, https://youtu.be/CtJ8Jjma5cM; and Freedom Prayer nonprofit at https://freedomprayer.org.

Therein is the problem: how to make it fit both audiences without putting one to sleep and frustrating the other. We humans are so complex.

To make it flexible in that way, I have done three things. First, the first two chapters lay out the problem and outline Paul's response to the Corinthian version of that problem. Second, the next eight chapters come in pairs. The first in each pair gives background information on that particular spiritual concept described by Paul in his corrective to the Corinthians. The second gives a quick background summary of the paired one, and then moves to practical application tips and approaches. And finally, for the things that might seem hopelessly boring to most and necessary to the rest, I have provided appendices that are referenced where applicable throughout the book.

I urge you to read chapters 1 and 2. I hope that you will see yourself there, and then you can decide how you will move through the rest of the book. I hope you, too, will exclaim, "That explains it! Thank you so much."

Andy Reese

Introduction

The Burning Plane

It was 1988, and I was daydreaming and gazing out the window of a small twin-prop plane on approach to Nashville. Suddenly, a woman across the aisle shrieked, "The plane is on fire! The plane IS. ON. FIRE!" That is when I first began to learn about gifting and finding God's purpose for my life.

It probably took such an event to wake me up. In the terminal prior to takeoff, I had been having a complaint session with God. I said something bratty like, "Am I supposed to go into full-time ministry or not? How am I supposed to know? Jesus had a book written about Him—not fair!" I continued in that vein for most of the flight. Just before the scheduled landing, I heard the screaming.

I frantically leaned across the aisle, looked past the woman, and saw flames and smoke streaming from the engine. The plane lurched as everyone else leaned, too. Fear shot through the passengers like a lightning bolt. There were shouts, lots of murmuring, a woman calming her daughter, and someone crying. It didn't help that the copilot pulled the curtain back, walked halfway down the aisle, looked out the window, and exclaimed, "Oh sh%#!" That is not what you want to hear from the pilot at a time like this. My stomach knotted.

Then a sudden calm came over me.

On takeoff, God had begun to answer my complaining with the fact that He had a book written about me, too. All my days and even my hairs are numbered (I'm less trouble than most of you), all my tears are in His bottle, and I was known before I was created (see Psalm 139:16; 56:8; Romans 8:29). He wisely hadn't laid out all the details and steps for me. I'm the type who would have run off and tried to do them.

That is when the scream punctuated the conversation. And He simply seemed to whisper, *Oh, and it's not written that you are going to die today.*

I considered bargaining about not being injured either but thought better of it. So I blurted out something hopelessly awkward like, "Don't worry. We are all going to be okay." I got a few well-earned incredulous looks.

The runway approach took forever, and we had a rough, roller coaster landing with lots of white-knuckled gasps. We stopped abruptly amid siren-screaming fire trucks and foam that was spewing onto the airplane engine. We quickly exited, moved to a safe distance, and sat in the grass on the runway's edge while they—ever so slowly—found a bus and had it cleared through security to come get us.

As I sat there, God began to talk to me. The thoughts came faster than I could process right then, but they seemed to be stored for me. That 45-minute wait changed almost everything I had thought or believed about gifting and purpose. It served as the basis and impetus for writing this book. It has proven itself true over 35 years, and I'm certain that will continue.

Here is what I learned on that runway that has filled out over the years. I'll save you the fire, screaming, and the rough landing. So let's go.

We Have a Problem

The conversation went something like this.

I was talking with a deeply spiritual and highly energetic young woman after a college group meeting. She told me about the latest personality test she had taken.

She said, "Wow, I finally understand my personality. I'm *not* crazy!"

She might still be crazy, I thought with a friendly smile, *but now she's happy about it.*

And I said, "That's great! That personality type sure seems to fit you. Now you know who you are! Oh ta-da!" Immediately a sort of icy chill came over her face. She looked away for a long second. When she looked back at me, her eyes were misty.

"Oh," she whispered. "You know, Andy. You know. We've talked about all this. That personality test doesn't tell me what I'm made for, only what I'm like. I think only God can show me my gifting and purpose, and I don't know why He won't!"

With growing angst, I asked, "I thought you had looked into all that. What happened?" Her eyes became fiery.

"Every answer I find seems to be unhelpful and contradicts every other answer. 'Spiritual gifts' seem to be sort of a Christian inside joke. I need to pick a major next week, and I need answers. Where is God in all this anyway?"

I hated "that" conversation. I lamely said something to her like, "I'm so sorry. You're right. I bet there is more there than what you're experiencing. I'm not satisfied because I don't understand spiritual gifts, either. I guess I sort of let it all go years ago. How about this—let's both look into the topic more and get back together."

She smiled weakly and said, "Okay, Andy. Great. Let me know what you think. I'd really like to have an answer to that question. I'll hold you to it!"

If that conversation had been an isolated incident, there would be no need for a book like this. A bit of counseling or spiritual direction, and all would be well. But reality is far, far from that scenario. Her summary of both the state of affairs at that time across the Church and its impact on individuals was spot on.

And that description still is true today. In the fall of 2021 and again in the spring of 2022, I spoke about spiritual gifting to two classes of about seventy students each at Lipscomb University, a fairly conservative Christian institution. At the beginning of my talk, I took a poll.

The first question was, "On a scale of one to five, how comfortable are you that you have a pretty good understanding of your 'spiritual gifting'—however you define it?"

I explained a vote of one meant "I have no clue about my spiritual gifting" and five meant "I am completely confident in my God-given spiritual gifting."

For the first class, I asked for a show of hands at "one." Maybe sixty percent raised their hands. When I asked about two . . . three . . . four, almost no one raised a hand. Okay . . . five!? Very few raised their hands for any number other than one! What?

I started over by defining zero to mean, "I don't have any real idea what that term actually means, much less what my giftings are." Then I got raised hands . . . and pained looks. The average score across the students in the first survey was just above 0.5—meaning most were clueless about spiritual gifts in general and their ap-plicability to their personal lives. The average in the second class was just above 1.0.

In each case, after a brief overview of the subject using the under-standing I'll describe in this book, I asked, "On a scale of one to five, how important do you feel it might be to understand your gifting package?" While I know it was a bit of a setup, the averages to that question were just above 4.2. That gap, between an understanding ranked 0.5 or 1.0 and a 4.2 informed desire, is the problem I am addressing in this book.

And this gap doesn't just exist among college students. Dr. Larry Gilbert, president of ChurchGrowth.org, surveyed 72 church-going adults, asking, "What is your spiritual gift?" Only 15 answered with what could be considered a valid name for any sort of spiritual gift, and 22 gave no response. Most amazing was that 28 listed their gift with a term that was nowhere in Scripture; and others listed fruit of the Spirit.[1]

I have spoken to business professionals, pastors of various stripes, professors, Sunday school classes, and incessantly to my friends about this subject. Among those who had even thought about it seriously (maybe fifty percent), none felt very comfortable with their current understanding even if they could give an answer that had a biblical name.

And you. What might your answer be? It's okay to be unsure. Welcome to the confused family!

I find that mix of disinterested, hopeful, confused, ambivalent, and disappointed desire for more understanding of and experience with spiritual giftings to be a near universal reality. Somewhere in our past and our minds, we have believed there must be something substantial and important to incorporate in our lives on the subject of spiritual gifts. But within our lives and behaviors, little of actual substance exists. An unmet longing for meaningful experience in the related areas of spiritual gifting, purposeful Christian living, and God-connection plays as insipid background music within the lives of most Christians I know. The older are just more inured to this unfulfilled longing than the young.

The saddest part to me is the widespread resignation. Is that really God's plan? I don't think so. And those who have grasped the concepts in this book would agree.

Spiritual Gifting Summary

It has been enlightening for others to hold up a mirror to allow each of us to see our church background and its beliefs and how those beliefs compare to others. But before I describe that "confused family" and its broad spectrum of beliefs about spiritual gifting, I wanted to give you a quick summary of what is generally meant when people mention the term *spiritual gifts*—a jumpstart into this subject. Here are the three major places in Scripture that, by general Church consensus, provide the listings that many have termed "spiritual gifts." I have inserted basic Greek terms for consistency in translation.* Take a quick look, and the rest of the chapter's discussion will be more clearly understood. Note in particular the wording Paul uses to describe each list.

1. Romans 12:6–8 states there are seven (*charisma*) gifts or functions performed by a gifted individual seeing through that gift's lens and feeling that motivation: prophecy, serving, teaching, exhorting, giving, leading, and showing mercy. First Peter 4:10–11 succinctly partners with Paul's verses stating there are two categories of gifts (speaking and serving) in the "many colored" grace of God.
2. Ephesians 4:11–12 gives five equipping ministry (*diakonia*) positions in the Body of Christ: apostle, prophet, evangelist, pastor, and teacher. In this passage, Paul clearly states that each of us has a current job or ministry and a growing career path measured out to us by Jesus—the head of the Body.

---

*To avoid confusion, where appropriate, I will refer parenthetically to the singular and most common expression of each Greek word, regardless of its Greek part of speech, tense, or cognate form, though such forms were taken into account in translation.

3. First Corinthians 12:8–10 lists nine "manifestations" (*phanerosis*) of the Spirit: tongues, interpretation of tongues, prophecy, word of knowledge, discerning of spirits, word of wisdom, gifts of healings, miracles, and faith. These are sometimes termed gifts, or miraculous gifts, of the Spirit. They can best be thought of as power tools to assist in the work of God.

4. Throughout Scripture, we might notice the often hidden work of the Father (*energema*) to steer and resource His children who love Him and are working according to His purposes in and through them (see Romans 8:28).

With that quick summary (don't worry, there is much more on these four later), let's now look at the understanding of spiritual gifts across the Church spectrum.

Spiritual Gifts—The Situation across the Church

I have found it important to gain a quick appreciation of the diversity of beliefs and practices concerning spiritual gifts across the Church. The definition of "gifting" seems to be institutionalized in several different ways. Author Wayne Grudem oversaw the writing of an interesting book documenting the range of beliefs concerning whether the 1 Corinthians 12 manifestations of the Spirit (not necessarily synonymous with spiritual gifts—see the four summaries previously given) are valid for today.[2] In each case, a scholar representing a particular position on the broader Church spectrum develops and supports the strongest argument for his or her beliefs while the others develop counterarguments, which are then also countered. The book convincingly demonstrates at least one thing: Brilliant scholars can come to thoughtful yet opposite conclusions on the topic of manifestations of the Spirit—and probably the wider topic of gifting covered in this book as well.

Let's use a visual guide (which I've called the Spiritual Gift Spectrum) modified from Grudem's book that can help frame the wide range of spiritual gifts beliefs and practices, however each group defines them. In my 45 years as a Christian, I have fellowshipped with every major stopping place along this spectrum. From my experience, typical beliefs within each grouping described below are essentially correct—at least enough to help us understand the spectrum of beliefs. Within any named category, there will certainly be a church, group, or individual whose belief and practice better resembles another group.

I also need to state that I have come to deeply appreciate the puzzle pieces of truth that each expression of Christianity has found and deployed within their context. Over the years, when I observed the variety of beliefs and practices, I have repeatedly said to myself, "I love this about them!" So I want to ensure that these observations are not meant to be critical, but simply informational in nature.

Let's cover each coast, first starting with the left, more charismatic (Pentecostal and charismatic), end, then the right, more conservative (cessationist and conservative denominational), side—saving the vast center (nondenominational and evangelical) for last.

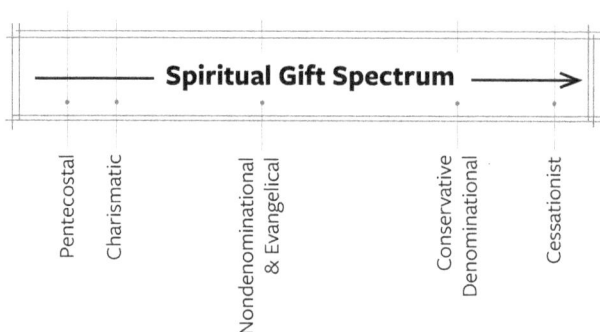

The Left Side of the Spectrum

On the left and moving toward the center is a continuum of various expressions of belief in the continuation of the manifestations and activity of the Holy Spirit from the Day of Pentecost until today.

They differ from each other, however, becoming less exclusive and rigorous in that belief as we move to the right and the more recently emerged expressions. To an outsider they might all fall under the broader practice-based title of "charismatic."

Pentecostalism

Pentecostalism grew out of the early twentieth-century Wesleyan-Holiness movement and the Azusa Street Revival of 1906. From a gifted perspective, Pentecostals tend to focus on the list of nine manifestations of the Holy Spirit listed in 1 Corinthians 12 as the definition of spiritual gifts (see the description earlier in this chapter entitled Spiritual Gifting Summary), with primary focus on the most common: tongues and sometimes prophecy. It is typically believed, based on their understanding of the accounts of Holy Spirit activity in the book of Acts and denominational history, that all believers will probably speak in tongues as a sign of being filled with (or being baptized in) the Holy Spirit. This typically happens at water baptism. Thus, they promote and give expression to the most common manifestations of the Spirit in 1 Corinthians 12.

The Charismatic Movement

The Charismatic Movement originated in the 1960s and exploded within the Church in the 1970s. The movement was marked by exuberance in worship and hunger for an experience of the Holy Spirit, both individually and corporately. Charismatics encourage believers to seek the gift of tongues, but as *a* sign, not *the* sign, of being baptized in the Holy Spirit.

The question "Are you Spirit-filled?" was a common one in those days. Charismatics also focused more on other manifestations, openly encouraging prophecy, words of knowledge, and others listed in the 1 Corinthians 12 passage in the description above. Across the movement, spiritual gifts are still largely recognized as the nine manifestations in 1 Corinthians 12. Many lives were deeply touched by this movement as the presence of God seemed to become more deeply and personally experienced. One gift this movement seemed to give to the Church worldwide was a strong expectation that the Spirit would move within and through the Church.

Coming on the heels of the Charismatic Movement, shifting still further toward the center of the spectrum, was the "Third Wave" (so named by C. Peter Wagner, also called Neo-Charismatic). The Third Wave began in the 1980s and continues today, merging with and maturing the earlier charismatic movements. Members accepted the charismatic concept of the manifestations and began to add a focus on topics such as spiritual warfare, faith, and miraculous healing. The leadership of John Wimber (1934–1997) of the Vineyard movement, the healing emphasis of Bill Johnson and Bethel Church in Redding, California (1996 to present), and the revivals in Toronto (1994 and following) and Pensacola (1995) are examples of popular front-and-center drivers for this movement.

In terms of understanding of gifting within the current day charismatics, there seems to be a maturation in the use of manifestations and a much-needed sort of "opening door" consideration of the other lists given by Paul and summarized above. Sam Storms, a Calvinist and former Wheaton College professor, might be considered a good example of leadership in this part of the spectrum. Storms provides examples of a more mature consideration of manifestations in his books *The Beginner's Guide to Spiritual Gifts* and *Practicing the Power*.[3]

The Right Side of the Spectrum

Let's now move to the right end of the figure to the more conservative portion of the Church.

Cessationist

At the right end of the spectrum are what have been termed, from a spiritual gift perspective, cessationists. Their definition of spiritual gifts is similar to the Pentecostals', yet they have come to opposite conclusions as to current-day usage. While they generally acknowledge that the nine 1 Corinthians 12 manifestations of the

Spirit did have an important purpose in the early Church, they believe that purpose has long since ceased, passing into history with the completion of the written canon of Scripture. Most cessationists would say that God can heal or work a miracle through anyone (or no one) anytime He desires, but that is different from, for example, the "gift of healing." Any broader view of spiritual gifts beyond the manifestations is not common.

Something I deeply appreciate about the far right (cessationist) end of the spectrum is an emphasis on the importance of proper biblical exegesis and hermeneutical understanding—both of which are sometimes lacking in other expressions. Typical of this approach when considering spiritual gifts are books by Church of Christ scholars Harvey Floyd, Tim Woodroof, and Leonard Allen.[4] Spanning 1981 to 2018, they seem to demonstrate what I have experienced in these settings as a growing interest in, and openness to, the Holy Spirit and spiritual gifts.

Conservative Denominational

If we move one stop to the left of cessationist, we enter the world of conservative, older line denominations (e.g., Baptist, Presbyterian, Methodist, Lutheran, Episcopalian, etc.). While the Charismatic Movement might have had an impact on individual churches in these groups, the general focus remains on sound Christian theology and practice—each group expressing its desire to raise mature, doctrinally sound believers in strong churches. From a spiritual gifting perspective, many appear as "functional" cessationists, meaning that the focus on spiritual gifts seems mostly muted; however, some of these churches or groups within them have a growing interest in the Holy Spirit and the gifts and manifestations of the Spirit.

The Spectrum Center: Nondenominational/Evangelical

As we move along the spectrum from both the right and left, we enter the vast "open prairie" of Christianity: nondenominational/evangelical. This group's varied definitions and beliefs on spiritual gifts are where things can get interesting. This expanse includes a large number of individual nondenominational churches, more "progressive" churches from various denominations, and church networks that believe in "continuationism" when it comes to spiritual gifts—meaning that spiritual gifts (however defined) have continued from Pentecost until today. Often there are various caveats, some of which I will summarize.

Multiple Gift Lists

Many megachurches, scholars, pastors, and spiritual thought leaders in public media within this group have taken a hard look at gifts. As they did so, they realized that the nine manifestations found in 1 Corinthians 12 are not the whole story. They assessed that their members were seeking, like my young friend at the beginning of this chapter, a sense of calling and purpose. And, lacking a scholarly consensus, many different interpretations and understandings of spiritual gifts have been developed. In so doing, each has had to make judgment calls on several critical components.

The first judgment call was to determine which items they would call "spiritual gifts" and what specific names they would give them. Most, but not all, derived their gift lists only from the three gift-list Scriptures summarized above: Romans 12, Ephesians 4, and 1 Corinthians 12. Second, each needed to determine what sacrifices, assumptions, and omissions were necessary to combine things into one coherent, noninflammatory list. And finally, each had to come up with explanations of various anomalies, such as repetition of some names, omission of others, and differing contexts within which the lists are given.

Some groups, for example, omit tongues or interpretation, saying that it is apparent who has those gifts and further mention can bring unnecessary division or misunderstanding. Others omit the nine manifestations but include all the others. Some, to make things fit, change various gift names. Some express sort of a selective cessationist belief, saying that some gifts have ceased. Some teach, for example, that apostles were only necessary to begin the Church, and their purpose and office died a long time ago—maybe taking prophets with them. Others include every use of the word *charisma* as a gift of the Spirit—which then includes, for example, celibacy. Some make up new gifts they considered implied within Scripture. Many variations.

Author C. Peter Wagner developed a popular spiritual gift approach that lists 28 spiritual gifts, extending beyond the Scriptures summarized above to include missionary, hospitality, voluntary poverty, celibacy, intercession, and leading worship. Author Rick Yohn combined all lists, renaming some things (e.g., a "word of knowledge" becomes "the gift of knowledge"). Author Robert Heidler describes kinds of gifting and assigns the source of the *charisma* gifts in Romans 12 to the Father. Darren Tyler[5] has written about the seven *charisma* gifts in Romans 12 and has chosen, for ease in his dynamic application, to rename them Visionary, Collaborator, Discerner, Encourager, Imparter, Guardian, and Responder. There are dozens of other authors who have written about spiritual gifts, generally in the same vein, with multiple variations on the list-modification theme.

A somewhat disconcerting internet search is the question "How many spiritual gifts are there?" The responses include What are the 22 spiritual gifts?; What are the 7 spiritual gifts?; The 12 gifts of the Holy Spirit; The 18 gifts of the Holy Spirit; 28 gifts to grow your church; and What are the 16 spiritual gifts? Many websites that people use to discover their gifts come with online tests that could help them quickly learn what they are—some with higher or lower probabilities included.

If you would like to experience this for yourself, I suggest that you search online for "spiritual gift tests" and take several. On a challenge from a friend, I tried that recently. The exercise was as disorienting to me as it was to my young friend so long ago. The results of my testing came out with all of the following being my spiritual gifts: creator, prophecy/knowledge/leadership, teaching/word of wisdom/discernment/tongues/exhortation, and shepherding/teaching. Thankfully, in no case was I gifted with celibacy or hospitality!

I'm probably naïve, but it seems painfully obvious that the Church has an immense problem—the gap between God's probable intent and our actual experience of "spiritual gifts."

The Intersection of Spiritual Gifts and Personality

Another complication (as if we needed another complication) is that there is some concern from academics about the purity of the results of spiritual gift tests. Statistical studies have been done relating personality test results and spiritual gift test results. In most cases, the concern is that spiritual gift tests may be measuring personality as much as or more than spiritual gifts—however defined. S. D. Choi, for example, found that gift questionnaires and personality inventories produced similar results. Gift characteristics and personality characteristics matched in a high percentage of the test takers—though those results differed between seminarians and Filipino sample sets.[6] He concluded that either the believer's personality was made to harmonize with his or her spiritual gifts, or spiritual gifts and personality traits are not essentially different. He theorized that at the time of conversion, the basic personality traits are made spiritually powerful.

Psychologist Dr. Kenneth Stone surmises in his detailed study that using spiritual gift tests is misleading and essentially useless. He believes that over half the questions are influenced by personality traits; therefore, the tests do not measure what they claim to measure. He states, "It is believed that these [spiritual gift] inventories are contaminated by personality traits, which account for the large amounts of error variance. This error may be hiding the distinct gifts."[7] His recommendation is that revising the tests would not produce better results, and "the best method of [gift] discovery seems to lie in the trial-and-error process" where mistakes are assumed, and leadership must be patient and tolerant of them.

If this topic is of interest, perhaps the most detailed information is developed within two complex websites. Over seventeen years, Jason Hawthorne developed detailed comparisons between a listing of 16 or 21 "spiritual gifts" and Isabel Myers's Myers-Briggs (MBTI) personality types—which she had originally named "Gifts Differing," an obvious reference to Romans 12. Aurelian, a pseudonym, also published detailed information on both the history of spiritual gifts and their potential connection to MBTI personality traits.[8] He summarized that opinions on the relationship between spiritual gifts and personality traits tend to fall into four categories:

1. They are often but not always related.
2. Both are important but are not related.
3. We confuse personality and gifts.
4. There is a one-to-one correlation of "personality types" and "spiritual gifts."

To address this issue, various churches have developed combined gift, personality, motivation, and even experience tests for congregants. The SHAPE profile of Rick Warren's Saddleback Church and the Network System of Bill Hybels's Willow Creek Community Church are the most well-known. Another site, Uniquely You,[9] ties one of several gift approaches (7 to 23 spiritual gifts) to the DISC personality profile system and generates lengthy reports on all combinations and permutations.

What is my takeaway? In some sense, the results of this research do not matter. I'll share more about this later, but I am one thing—one person. I have a gifting and a personality—I am spirit, soul, and body. The work of God in and through me does not need definition as much as it needs simple awareness and attention. God makes it easy if we simply do our best.

What about Me?

God is calling each of us to look past a particular denomination's or church's definition and teaching and ask ourselves what we believe and what that means to our Christian beliefs and walk. Ask yourself: Where do I fit into the spectrum of beliefs? How did I come to that understanding? How do my belief and practice square with Scripture? What is their fruit in my life? Most say that someone taught on it, they took a test, or they just believed that they were good at this or that—biblical name or not. Only a very small minority arrived at a sense of gifting via personal study, prayer, and self-observation.

Fewer yet have taken steps to exercise that gifting, and far fewer come into a sense of purpose based partially on that gifting.

It seems each of us also has a problem.

The Purpose of This Book

On that day so long ago with my young friend, I felt strongly that God's intention was not for me to offer a myriad of alternate explanations or tests on the topic of spiritual gifts, which I believed would invite more confusion into her life. Instead, it became clear to me that, like the Corinthians, we were asking the wrong question. We had been asking, "What are my spiritual gifts?" And God's answer through Paul is far wider and wiser than that question. He places spiritual gifts into a broader and more coherent context, creating a way for people to understand and engage with Him that is biblical, God-connecting, practical, and life transforming.

The remainder of this book is the result of a long trial-and-error process, of starting with a clean tabletop, few presuppositions, simple questions, soaking in Scripture, and years of developing and rejecting ideas that did not meet the four-part criteria. This book is also a synthesis of a hundred conversations—some going long into the night, some in class, some with scholars, and most with wise old friends.

The answer I feel I have arrived at is far better than the "What are my spiritual gifts?" question I asked so long ago. It meets my four criteria. It can be easily demonstrated in Scripture without recourse to stretching things. It draws us to active connection with each member of the Trinity. It has a simple and clear application. And it has been shown to change lives for the better.

So with sincere thanks for the many great insights of other writers and the pieces contributed by various expressions of Christianity on this subject, I push my own puzzle pieces to the center of the table and ask you to see if they fit, if they might be just the pieces you're looking for. Many have said they are. I hope you think so, too. These pieces are pretty revolutionary, I'm told. See what you think.

We need a revolution.

Paul's Analysis
of Spiritual Things

In the last chapter, we explored the current state of affairs within the Church concerning spiritual gifting, however it is defined. In this chapter, we will start with that clean tabletop mentioned in the last chapter and follow Scripture's clear and detailed discussion of things related to spiritual gifting and their implications for us both individually and for the Church.

Paul and the Corinthians

We would be wise to start our exploration of spiritual gifting the same place Paul did . . . with Plato. What!? Let me first explain, and then we'll get back to Plato.

The Corinthian church, founded by Paul, apparently asked his advice on several issues, including the church's disorderly meetings and the misuse of manifestations of the Holy Spirit—specifically tongues and prophecy. Intended by God for good, the outcome was a cacophony of tongues without interpretation, prophecy without mature content judgment, and people speaking on top of each other. Perhaps they had bigger issues.

In 1 Corinthians 12, Paul begins his corrective discourse and seems to do so in a strange way. He divides his answer into four distinct parts all combined under one heading, and each using the Greek word *diairesis* to describe his consideration of each of the four parts. To ensure we are tracking with Paul's careful choice of vocabulary, I have included only key verses, parenthetically inserted key words in their basic Greek form, and carefully expressed terms and phrases using a combination of translations and definitions contextually within the verses:*

> [1]Now, concerning things of the spirit [*pneumatikos*], brothers and sisters, I don't want you to be uninformed and ignorant. [4]There is a distinct division [*diairesis*] of grace-gifts [*charisma*], but the same Spirit. [5]There is a distinct division [*diairesis*] of ministries [*diakonia*], but the same Lord. [6]There is a distinct division [*diairesis*] of empowered effects [*energema*], but the same God who works all things in everyone. [7]On the other hand, each one is given the clearly visible manifestation [*phanerosis*] of the Spirit for the common good. [8]For to one is given. . . . [11]But the same Spirit empowers these things distinctly dividing [*diairesis*] to each individually as He wills.

Basically, Paul says that the felt concerns of the Corinthians may be about tongues, prophecy, and order in meetings, but those concerns are really a tiny part of a more critical topic. As discussed in chapter 1, they have asked the wrong question. He states, "Now concerning the things of the spirit [*pneumatikos*]† . . . I don't want you to be ignorant." He is saying that there is an important understanding of the broader and deeper "things of the spirit" that their concerns seem to have missed. Maybe we, too, have missed those things. Let's explore together and see.

*Just as a reminder from chapter 1, to avoid confusion, where appropriate, I will refer parenthetically to the singular and most common expression of each Greek word, regardless of its Greek part of speech, tense, or cognate form, though such forms were taken into account in translation.

†This word is translated "spiritual gifts" in many translations, though such an interpretation may tend to obscure Paul's actual point and purpose.

What are those things Paul appears to feel are critical to being God's people? In answer he lays out, in the passage quoted above, a four-part, Trinity-linked structure of these "things of the spirit." In so doing, he repeatedly uses the Greek word *diairesis* to describe how he developed and sees this structure. And he also declares that this structure is how they should think so that they are not ignorant.

I have taken pains to provide a one word "handle" for each of the four things of the spirit that closely approximates the Greek word and meaning. I will also do so for the subcomponents of each of the four. When, as we saw in the previous chapter with *charisma* gifts, we provide an imaginative and interpretative name to Paul's named things or their subsets, we are, in a sense, taking something that is multidimensional in name and reducing it to our own one-dimensional understanding. Calling prophecy "discernment" might be an example. Depth and breadth of meaning is lost or wanders from the truth, and the thing becomes sort of "plain vanilla." I'll try not to do that, even at the expense of cute or easy to remember naming conventions.

Things of the Spirit (Pneumatikos) Summary

Since this *pneumatikos* idea may be new to you, let me give a brief definition of each of these four things of the spirit mentioned by Paul in 1 Corinthians 12. I will further develop these definitions later but want to provide a brief summary of our destination here at the beginning to save you the temporary confusion that might arise as the journey is just beginning. These definitions have been derived from scriptural cross-references and examples, a wide variety of other sources, discussions across the Church spectrum, and experience.

Gifts (Charisma) and the Holy Spirit

> ▶ There is a distinct division [diairesis] of grace-gifts [charisma] but the same Spirit.
> ▶ Key verses: 1 Corinthians 12:4; Romans 12:3–8; 1 Peter 4:10–11

The Holy Spirit connects within and empowers individuals. The Holy Spirit provides a "gift" (*charisma*), which is a spiritual aptitude or enabling related to a basic or generic function within the Body of Christ. It could also be thought of as a lens through which I observe life, or a motivation in any situation. In Romans 12, Paul lists seven types or categories of *charisma* gifts: prophecy, serving, teaching, exhorting, giving, leading, and showing mercy.

Ministries (diakonia) and Jesus

▶ There is a distinct division [diairesis] of ministries [diakonia] but the same Lord.

▶ Key verses: 1 Corinthians 12:5; Ephesians 4:7–16

Jesus, the head (think "brain," not "boss"; it's an organism more than an organization) of the Body, empowers, works, and connects with every individual within His Body. We each have a "ministry" (*diakonia*) to which Jesus called and strengthens us that is both what we are currently doing and our long-term career that was envisioned by Jesus. Jesus describes how this works in multiple parables and statements about being faithful in little things, the talents and minas, and more. Jesus appoints mature individuals to five kinds of equipping roles to prepare others for their own ministries. These five named equipping ministries are apostle, prophet, evangelist, pastor, and teacher.

Effects (energema) and the Father

▶ There is a distinct division [diairesis] of empowered effects [energema] but the same God who works all things in everyone.

▶ Key verses: 1 Corinthians 12:6; Romans 8:28; 1 Corinthians 1:9; 3:6; 12:28

The Father works across the world, mostly in the background, to ensure that the right things happen in the right way at the right time. He does this by steering circumstances and people and providing the right resources in a timely way to produce the results and impact He intends to have on and through His children.

Manifestations of the Spirit (phanerosis)

▶ On the other hand, each one is given the clearly visible manifestation [phanerosis] of the Spirit for the common good. But the same

Spirit empowers these things distinctly, dividing [diairesis] to each individually as He wills.

▶ Key verses: 1 Corinthians 12:7–14:40

A manifestation (*phanerosis*) is a power intervention by the Holy Spirit into a life or situation—which may be a one-time thing (someone is healed), or ongoing—and can be at will (someone speaks in tongues). Paul lists nine categories of manifestations: tongues, interpretation of tongues, prophecy, word of knowledge, word of wisdom, discerning of spirits, gifts of healings, faith, and miracles. It is the outflowing of the Holy Spirit from within us, or upon us, for a specific purpose.

Now, back to Plato.

Paul's Diairesis Thinking

Notice in the 1 Corinthians 12 passage above that Paul uses the word *diairesis* four times to describe his assessment of each of the four parts of the things of the spirit (*phanerosis*). Understanding Paul's probable intention in use of that word is a key to sorting out truth about things of the spirit—and far more importantly, addressing the spiritual gift confusion and malaise in Corinth and within the Church today.

Diairesis is a Greek word that was probably invented, but certainly popularized, by Plato (428–348 BCE).[1] The term commonly carries a specific sense, formally or informally, of an ordered thought process to organize information for specific purposes. *Diairesis* is defined by Thayer as "a distinction arising from a different distribution to different persons."[2]

Formally or informally, in the method of *diairesis*, the goal is to obtain an organized and clear understanding of a topic. In its simple three-step form, one would

1. define the topic of analysis;
2. consider how to define and title the complete range of possible "class" members within that topic or subtopic; and

3. think deeply about each of the categories, patterns, uses, order, and meaning in terms of some final decision, distribution, or disposition based on the specific purpose of the *diairesis* analysis.

A form of the word *diairesis* is used only one other time in Scripture. It is the verb "divide," used in Luke 15:12, when the father of the prodigal son and older brother is faced with the exacting task of sorting his estate between his two sons—one who is departing. You can imagine the careful consideration he went through to enumerate, evaluate, divide, and distribute all his belongings. Did the prodigal son only get "liquid" assets? Sheep or barns wouldn't work on the road. How would he keep the estate functioning?

Many examples of the use of *diairesis* are referenced in ancient literature, including organizing and describing military organization, dissection, division of spoils, grammar, rhetoric, and finance. Today we do not call this way of thinking anything in particular; however, you and I have encountered this thought process hundreds of times for things such as the organization of grocery store aisles, Enneagram personality types, organization of the animal kingdom, and every child sitting on the floor sorting out a Halloween haul.

It is helpful to understand *diairesis* by comparing its usage to the use of the English word "appraisal." Appraisal carries both a formal and informal meaning but is always colored by a special emphasis. Appraisal is used formally to describe the process that is followed when value is assigned to things like houses, cars, diamonds, etc. A trained individual follows a rigid procedure to arrive at a value estimate. But appraisal is also used less formally to imply a particular focused and analytical sense of attention. Your parents may observe your friends, but they appraise your potential mate. *Diairesis* is like that in the sense of implied special meaning even if a formal process has not been entered into.

The question is, Might Paul have used this thought process, in a formal or informal sense, when assessing things of the spirit, and, if so, how might that color our assessment of what he is saying to the Corinthians—and to us?

The evidence seems clear that he could and did. Paul was a child prodigy steeped in Greek culture.[3] He studied in the school of Rabbi Gamaliel. He was a "Pharisee of Pharisees" and persecutor of this wayward sect of followers of Jesus (see Philippians 3:4–6).

Then he encounters the risen Christ! It seems that the shocked and blinded young Pharisee was shaken to the core, and that much of his structured teaching probably grew out of time spent in Damascus and Arabia seeking to understand the implications and meaning of both the Old Testament prophecy and the new Gospel of Christ (see Galatians 1:13–17). Paul was a stickler for truth—detailed, long-winded truth, as story after story attests (see Galatians 2:2; Acts 20:7–12; 17:16–34; 26:24). He was undeniably "that guy" you did not want to invite to a cocktail party!

In summary, it seems that in Paul's mind the Corinthians needed to see the big picture into which they could put their issues. And that big picture could best be grasped through an ordered discussion using, formally or more informally, the thought process of *diairesis* concerning things of the spirit. And in this letter, he said so—four times.

Implications of Paul's Diairesis Thinking

If Paul used a *diairesis* type of thought process concerning the structure of the spirit world (*pneumatikos*), then there are certain clear implications about how we might consider what has been written by him.

First and foremost, Paul's *diairesis* thinking implies that the various lists are not simply examples of items in each category, as some have thought, but they are meant to deliberately and fully, however briefly, define and provide a heading name for the category. This implies, for example, that the gift (*charisma*) listing of seven items in Romans 12 would be best understood as intended to categorize and give encompassing titles to the complete range of the *charisma* component of things of the spirit.* And this type of categorization would also, in some way, be true of the other three categories—*diakonia* ministries in Ephesians 4, *energema* empowered effects in many places in Scripture, especially Acts, and *phanerosis* manifestations in 1 Corinthians 12.

Looking through the lens of such analysis, as we will do in the subsequent chapters, we will begin to see that the realities of Paul's groupings emerge as genius, as inspired, and as putting these things easily within our understanding and reach. And we begin to understand that the question the Corinthians should have asked was, How do we relate intimately with the members of the Trinity, and in doing so, find powerful keys to understanding and walking in our life's purposes?

Paul's Structure Is Not Mysterious

We might be tempted to place Paul's four-part structure into some kind of hyperspiritual box. But think outside the box for a moment. Paul's analysis of the structure of the spirit world is not some mysterious one-of-a-kind heavenly structure. In fact, we could equally apply this four-part description to nearly any organization with a mission. Let's think about, for example, how we might describe the organizational workings of a hospital using "Paul-speak." We might say the hospital is structured as four basic components.

Basic *skill sets/talents* (*charisma*) are necessary for the hospital to run smoothly. A personnel director (Holy Spirit) addresses these various skills when he describes the types of roles people play: "We have medical, technician, administration, groundskeeping, and several other skill categories here at the hospital."

Various positions (*diakonia*) in the organizational chart are specifically identified that need these diverse skill sets/talents at different levels of experience. The hospital director (Jesus) makes this determination of need, and He hires people to fill those roles. He, as the head of the hospital, says, "We are going to need three new

---

*Generally listed as prophecy, service, one who teaches, one who exhorts, one who gives, one who leads, and one who shows mercy.

pediatricians, five nurses, and an X-ray technician for the growing children's wing next year. Here are the specific job descriptions."

The hospital has various *goals, outcomes, and needs (energema)*. The chairman of the board (the Father) works behind the scenes to make the hospital and each employee successful, stepping in with resources, permissions, advice, and connections—whatever is necessary to bring about the desired outcome. He tells the board, "Next year we will need two million in additional funding to finish the children's wing construction. And I'd like to send Doctor Jones to that conference in France to talk about the new techniques we supported him in developing. It's a great opportunity. Let's make it happen for him."

Part of helping make each employee successful is to ensure each person has timely access to the *equipment and technology (phanerosis)* they need to get the job done—one needs a scanner, another needs computer resources, another needs floor polishers, another financial analysis tools, etc. Maybe almost everyone needs a phone and a computer. Some things are used less frequently but are still necessary. So the personnel director (Holy Spirit) makes sure each new hire and department has what they need, when they need it.

We could give these four components business names instead of Bible names (basic skills/talents and specific job positions, executive sponsorship, and technology support), and few of us would quibble about the understanding and application in any number of situations. The organization called the Body of Christ needs these four kinds of things, too—gifts, ministries, effects, and manifestations.

When we discover how to incorporate this approach into our everyday thinking about our Christian life and relationship with the Godhead, we begin to discern the voices and observe the actions of each member of the Trinity in new ways. These new ways begin to bring our lives into more purposeful focus. We find that this understanding opens a door of connection and direction that bears lifelong fruit.

A set of concerns or alternate interpretations might be expressed about these deductions and their formulation. Appendix A discusses these objections, concerns, and my conclusions. Let me simply state that I believe that Paul's unambiguous use of a four-part *diairesis* description of his thinking—along with his later expansion of things of the spirit in other epistles—is the key to his answer to the Corinthians and must be given significant precedence in our thinking. It was in his.

I kept the most important thing for last.

If You Only Remember One Thing

You may have noted that Paul matches each of the things of the spirit to a member of the Trinity. Why is this so? Understanding this idea may be the most important thing you get out of this book.

Jesus said to the Pharisees, "You examine the Scriptures because you think that in them you have eternal life; and it is those very Scriptures that testify about Me; and yet you are unwilling to come to Me so that you may have life" (John 5:39–40). What a critical exposé of "religion" versus "relationship." Paul makes the same statement when he begins listing his religious resume and then, maybe surprising some of his readers, ends by calling all his accomplishments "rubbish" when compared to knowing and intimately relating to Christ.

> But whatever things were gain to me, these things I have counted as loss because of Christ. More than that, I count all things to be loss in view of the surpassing value of knowing Christ Jesus my Lord, for whom I have suffered the loss of all things, and count them mere rubbish.
>
> Philippians 3:7–8

We must get this about gifts and the rest of the *pneumatikos* components, too. We may have thought of spiritual gifts as something that God gives to us, like some celestial Santa secretly dropping presents under the tree at midnight. And we go off to use them in our self-developed (and often self-named) ministry. Nothing could be further from the truth. Paul makes it crystal clear that God is interested in inviting us into family relationship and in doing things with and through us—with each member of the Trinity and some part of the business of the Kingdom of God, the *pneumatikos*, assigned to us.

This is clearly how Jesus lived: Spirit-filled and connected to the Father (see John 5:19, 30; 6:38; 8:28; 12:49–50; 14:10). Jesus promises the Holy Spirit to His believers when He states, "But I tell you the truth: it is to your advantage that I am leaving; for if I do not leave, the Helper will not come to you; but if I go, I will send Him to you" (John 16:7). The Holy Spirit is described in many ways with multiple roles. But in that same conversation, Jesus also says something crazy amazing. "If anyone loves Me, he will follow My word; and My Father will love him, and We will come to him and make Our dwelling with him" (John 14:23). Imagine that! The Trinity chooses to move in with us. Right there, inside each of us. Maybe I should clean up the mess—guests are moving in. Okay then!

Spiritual giftedness and finding purpose are about connection. If you find that a bit intimidating, then welcome! But know this: God knows our weaknesses, awkwardness, and insecurity about all this, and yet He makes merciful and gentle provision for us. He will help us clean up the house. We will talk much more and often about that as we enter each of the four *pneumatikos* things of the spirit in the next chapters.

The Diagram

Okay, I'm geeky! I like flow charts and diagrams to reinforce and clarify ideas. I apologize to those of you who may passionately hate them. It's okay to skip to the next chapter rather than be triggered!

Now, for the rest of us . . . Paul organized things for clarity, and a diagram seems an easy way to understand and build on his analysis. The diagram below is a depiction of Paul's *diairesis* analysis as we have discussed it so far. We will build the next layer as we go.

The top level is the umbrella term Paul is concerned with, the things of the spirit (*pneumatikos*). In the second level, we see that he has broken that term into its four constituent parts: gifts (*charisma*), ministries (*diakonia*), effects (*energema*), and manifestations (*phanerosis*). In the following chapters, we will unveil the amazing truth within the next levels and show how Paul's revelation can help define your purpose and propel your spiritual life.

As stated several times, my hope is that you will find our upcoming discussion biblical, practical, transformative, and God-connecting. That has been my experience, as well as the experience of many others. That is also my prayer.

With that, let's find your spiritual gift (*charisma*). Ready?

	Level 1 Things of the Spirit *pneumatikos* 1 Cor 12:1		
1 Cor 12:4 ▼ Spirit	1 Cor 12:5 ▼ Jesus	1 Cor 12:6 ▼ Father	1 Cor 12:7 ▼ Spirit
Level 2 Gifts *charisma*	**Level 2** Ministries *diakonia*	**Level 2** Effects *energema*	**Level 2** Manifestations *phanerosis*

The Spirit and Charisma Gifts

In the last chapter, we looked at Paul's four-part grace structure called *pneumatikos,* or things of the spirit: gifts (*charisma*), ministries (*diakonia*), effects (*energema*), and manifestations (*phanerosis*).* It seems clear that this organization was configured as an outcome of Paul's prayerful consideration and careful analysis. There is nothing mysterious about that, especially since it was Paul's intent to help remove Corinthian ignorance concerning these things of the spirit. We are the beneficiaries of the Corinthian ignorance, as it is likely ours as well.

Our next step in gaining keys to finding connection and our God-given purposes is to explore the first part of the four-part structure: *charisma* gifts. This topic is divided into two chapters. The first is understanding what gifts are and how God has arranged and organized them for understanding and application, and the second is a practical application tool using that arrangement in our lives.

---

*For the rest of the book, I will endeavor to use these four words exclusively in a one-to-one match: *charisma*/gift, *diakonia*/ministry, *energema*/effect, and *phanerosis*/manifestation.

But before we plunge into Scripture and analysis, I want to tell a story. It illustrates a key concept that will take a lot of pressure off the whole idea of "finding my gift."

I have a leadership-gifted son. He does not think in those terms, but everyone else does. His wife, a nutrition expert and trainer, and he had just opened a gymnasium when the March 2020 tornado hit Nashville. The gym was located near the storm track, which also passed through a poor, and now devastated, neighborhood. When he saw that the neighborhood was without immediate aid, even though other parts of town were being helped, he was stirred to action.

As he was the head of the local bartenders guild that year, he sent out an all-points bulletin to the bartenders asking for them to report to the gym with chainsaws the next day at 7:30 a.m. He also called me to see if my church could help. It is the kind of church that jumps at that sort of thing. So at 7:30 a.m. the next day, two groups of about forty each showed up, bartenders and Church of Christ churchmen (yup).

They were paired off and sent into the neighborhood. They cleared blocks of mess, moved trees, stopped plumbing leaks, boarded up windows, and made great new friendships. A police-woman from the neighborhood who was weeping with joy hugged me and shook her head. She said that it looked like Jesus to her. My son later told me that that workday was both the hardest and most rewarding thing he had ever done.

Operating in the center of your *charisma* is like that. He is one who leads. He can't help it. God wants you to understand and live in your own gifting. You are gifted. . . . You are. You can't help it, either. And because God is active in bringing you into the power of your gifting, even with a limited amount of understanding, when you simply do what seems right—that which captures your attention, turns your head, or maybe makes your blood boil—then you will stumble into your gifting. This will happen even if you aren't sure it is even a "thing" and certainly could never name it. Oh, the Father's mercy!

Okay, let's develop an understanding of *charisma* gifts.

Paul and Peter on Charisma

In Romans 12, Paul provides the *diairesis* analysis details of his 1 Corinthians 12 mention of *charisma* gifts:

> ³For through the grace [*charis*] given to me I say to everyone among you not to think more highly of himself than he ought to think; but to think so as to have sound judgment, as God has allotted to each a measure of faith. ⁴For just as we have many parts in one body and all the body's parts do not have the same function [*praxis*], ⁵so we, who are many, are one body in Christ, and individually parts of one of another. ⁶However, since we have gifts [*charisma*] that differ according to the grace [*charis*] given to us, each of us is to use them properly: if prophecy, in proportion to one's faith; ⁷if service, in the act of serving; or the one who teaches, in the act of teaching; ⁸or the one who exhorts, in the work of exhortation; the one who gives, with generosity; the one who is in leadership, with diligence; the one who shows mercy, with cheerfulness.
>
> Romans 12:3–8

Peter, who thought Paul might be too complex or wordy at times (see 2 Peter 3:16), in two short verses provides his own insight into *charisma* gifts, efficiently compacting Paul's arrangement into the categories of serving and speaking gifts and providing additional insights:

> As each one has received a special gift [*charisma*], employ it in serving [*diakonia*] one another as good stewards of the multicolored [*poikilos*] grace of God. Whoever speaks is to do so as one who is speaking actual words of God; whoever serves is to do so as one who is serving by the strength which God supplies; so that in all things God may be glorified through Jesus Christ, to whom belongs the glory and dominion forever and ever. Amen.
>
> 1 Peter 4:10–11

Keys to Understanding Charisma Gifts

Let's combine the points in Peter's and then Paul's narratives to look at nine important keys to understanding *charisma* gifts and finding our own gifting. Then, in the next chapter, we'll quickly assemble those puzzle pieces into a simple and effective tool for determining our own *charisma* gifting. Skip ahead if you'd like, but I think these keys will help you better see God's amazing pattern and plan. Refer back to the verses given above as you read through the keys.

Key 1: There Are Seven Charisma Gifts in Two General Categories

In 1 Peter 4, Peter implies that all gifting falls into one of two general categories: speaking or serving. Peter also literally describes *charisma* gifts as the "multicolored" (*poikilos*) grace of God. Paul, in Romans 12, lists seven *charisma* gifts. Notice that these seven *charisma* gifts fall into Peter's two categories—three in each, with *leading* being some of both. Speaking gifts are prophecy, teaching, exhorting. Serving gifts are mercy, serving, and giving.*

To give us a quick understanding of each of the seven *charisma* gifts, here is a brief one-line synopsis of each of them. Each is expressed in terms of the issue in the body the gifted one sees and seeks to alleviate. More detail is given in the next chapter (when you consider your own gifting) and in Appendix B.

> Leading: eliminating group dysfunction and bringing vision and order
>
> Prophecy: eliminating what is wrong and bringing what is right
>
> Teaching: eliminating what is ignorant or false and bringing vital, living truth
>
> Exhorting: eliminating wounding and confusion and bringing healing and purpose
>
> Giving: eliminating lack and investing in high quality gain
>
> Serving: eliminating physical needs and focusing on "get-er-done"
>
> Mercy: eliminating pain and sadness and investing in joy

*In the list of one-word titles I have chosen to use for the gifts, there is a bit of mixture between nouns and gerunds, but it has been done that way to maximize clarity and to ensure there is no confusion between the person and the gift.

Key 2: We Each Have a Gift

Peter says that each one has received a *charisma* gift. Nobody is left out. He makes no distinction based on spiritual experience or maturity—or anything. There is no planned unemployment in the Body of Christ. You may be confused, uninstructed, uninterested, or uninitiated in gifts, but that does not mean you do not have a *charisma* gift. It only means that you do not know that you have one, or you do not know what it is. It is a bit like a high school student who has yet to give a name to his or her innate talents and aptitude toward a career or life-focus direction. And importantly, those talents are already within the high school student just as the *charisma* gift is within you, for life.

Key 3: Our Gift Is Our General Function in the Body

Paul says our gift defines our generic function (*praxis*) in the Body of Christ—I am "one who" (Romans 12:3–4). In verse 4, Paul mixes analogies and comments that we are each a "body part." As such, each has a specific "function" in the Body. First Corinthians 12:12–27 goes into great detail on this idea (see Key 5 below) correcting the issue of both self-pride and self-deprecation based on our assigned "body part" or "function."

Thayer defines *praxis* (function) as "a doing, a mode of acting."[1] So it seems that *charisma* is God's impartation of a specific spiritual grace into someone to give them a specific aptitude, ability, function, lens, or motivation. I tend to see things around me through a specifically colored lens, from a certain perspective. And that perspective motivates me to actions that are coherent with my gifting. My *charisma* gift means I can grow to be good at something in the Body, and it means I have a basic God-imparted aptitude or ability. That ability, when combined with my natural talents and strengths, can then be used in a near infinite number of ways in its many expressions as ministry (*diakonia*) jobs from Jesus.

What if we are disobedient to that tug of God? Will we change or lose our gifting? I don't think so. In my experience, we just "go around the mountain again," arriving back at the place of calling.

Paul says, "The gifts and the calling of God are irrevocable [without repentance]" (Romans 11:29). Our primary color will always remain the same. The works God has for us to do on the earth are our responsibility (see Ephesians 2:10).

Key 4: We Have One Charisma Gift

These verses imply that I have one *charisma* gift because there is only one "me." Does that seem limiting? Compare that idea to personality types. If I were to ask the question, "How many personality types do I have?" then, unless a person suffers from advanced dissociation, most would agree that we each have a single personality. I might ask you which Myers-Briggs Type you are, or what your Enneagram number is; however, for each of those indicator types, it is your one-and-only soul that is being classified and described—one thing, no matter how complex. Someone may appear to act like another Enneagram type under certain circumstances, but they have one, and only one, home type. And having only one personality is not limiting; it is human. So, too, we each are something spiritually. That is a basic understanding of *charisma*.

Let's expand on this point for a minute. Am I stuck doing only one thing? No! We all occasionally serve in different areas simply because we are Christians and Scripture tells us to. For example, my wife and I spent over a year serving our wonderful mothers, both in their nineties, during the initial COVID-19 outbreak. Such care would not reflect either of our gifting focuses, but it was an opportunity to do the right thing. And because of their great susceptibility, isolation was of paramount importance.

It is a mistake to think that you are not to help when a need presents itself that does not fit within your area of gifting. Often, in the wisdom of God, that kind sacrifice takes us down a hallway and opens a door we could not have seen otherwise.

So the *charisma* gift (focused on one of seven named functional types) stays the same even as it grows in strength, breadth, and authority—just as is the experience of our soul. Honestly, if you had to start over from time to time with a new *charisma*, it would be difficult and deflating. There is one you—and that's a good thing.

Key 5: We Are Stewards Serving, Not Owners Presiding

Peter states that we are to be "good stewards" (not owners) of the gifts we have been given (see 1 Peter 4:10). In 1 Corinthians 4:2, Paul makes it clear that stewards of the things of God should be trustworthy. Later in the same letter, he cements this idea with the words "What do you have that you did not receive? And if you did receive it, why do you boast as if you had not received it?" (1 Corinthians 4:7). Being a steward implies that we remain accountable and connected to the owner. Peter instructs that we are to employ *charisma* gifts in serving one another, and they should be employed in such a way that the "Owner" may be glorified (see 1 Peter 4:11).

This exhortation contains a safety factor. From the world's perspective, our gifting and talent is encouraged to be used to become respected by men. We are urged to be successful in our careers and to be wealthy, important, recognized, and dominant. When gifts and manifestations of the Spirit are used for showmanship or to build an audience, even partially, then people become connected to the gifted person and less so to God. And the beginnings of these other people's gift or manifestation realization can be quashed. They can think, "I could never be that great."

In the opposite direction from pride is the problem of fear or slackness. There are matching, but subtly different, parables given by Jesus where virgins have (or do not have) extra oil, or a steward is given some of the owner's wealth to invest (see Matthew 25:1–30; Luke 19:12–26). Among them, only the virgins who did not trouble themselves to take along extra oil, or the steward who didn't know the owner and fearfully hid his gift, were punished. All the rest probably made mistakes in certain ways—but their mistakes were never mentioned in the parables. Mis*takes* are not a problem with God—He just gives you another take.

Giftings and the attitudes associated with them are designed to work together to create a culture of honor. In 1 Corinthians 12:18–25, after the things of the spirit discussion, Paul turns to the attitude issues in the Corinthian church that probably helped lead to the show-off culture. Paul says we are to have the *same* care but *differing* honor for one another. When the Church begins to focus honor, the foot-washing kind, on the serving gifts and the least among us, the result is amazing unity within the Body, flowing grace, and a sense of awe. The healthy and mature speaking gifts rarely need such deliberate and public honor-giving—it mostly comes with the gifting.

Key 6: Our Gift Is Not Our Identity

I need to quash a common bad habit that we Christians often employ when we discuss gifting. It is common when someone is teaching on gifts to identify people by their gift. We might say, "She is a mercy" or "I'm a giver." But my *charisma* is not my identity. I am a child of God who has been gifted. When someone says, "I'm a plumber," it defines something about them. But that something is probably not the thing their parent, partner, or pal loves most about them. Paul is subtly clear in most of his wording in the Romans verses above—a person is "the one" performing this function (e.g., "one who shows mercy"), but he or she is not the function. You're still the one!

Key 7: Our Gifts Are Empowered by God

Peter makes it very clear that God the Father is the one who strengthens, empowers, and "energizes" (remember *energema*) both the speaking and serving gifts to accomplish His will (see 1 Peter 4:11). As we employ our gifting, we do so in the fear of the Lord with the sure knowledge that it is He who works in and through us. This means we live and move in God. We learn, however slowly, to honor the flow of that Spirit-river that is within us and pours out into the world (see John 7:38). Our own strength is a poor copy of the real thing—maybe good, but never glorious. We resort to it when we fear God won't come through or when waiting on His timing and way feels hard. Jude describes the ones who are such self-empowered individuals as merely natural (see Jude 1:19). Merely. Natural. That is a major put-down in the Kingdom of God. Don't go there.

Key 8: There Is a Logical Charisma Gift Structure

As mentioned in Key 1, Peter states that there are two overall categories of *charisma* gifts—to speak and to serve—and seven general types of *charisma*: prophecy, serving, teaching, exhorting, giving, leading, mercy. A common question is, "Are there really only seven (or worse, two) kinds of people?" Not even close.

In the *diairesis* consideration that we discussed in the last chapter, an objective in each categorical analysis is to fully define that division; to cover it end to end using titles or names for the different classes or groups of things. And thus, every item (or person, in this case) belonging to that overall category could be placed under a heading. Think like Plato for a moment and do your own gift *diairesis* analysis.

Ask this question: What kind of verbal input (e.g., Peter's speaking) does every person need from time to time? Well, everyone, especially when young or ignorant about something, needs instruction. This instruction (teaching) does not need to be done in a formal classroom setting. It can be timely and impromptu information sharing. We all need to be taught. And if someone is confused about their next steps or strays in a harmful direction, they need correction and redirection from someone who clearly sees their danger. Let's call that prophecy (in Paul's words). And, finally, everyone needs encouragement when they are lagging or need a boost. This is true both in general and when that encouragement is specifically targeted toward a defined purpose. Let's call that exhorting. Apostle Paul, using his exhorting gift (see Acts 20:1–2), says that in life, people need three kinds of speaking: teaching, prophecy, and exhorting.

While there are many forms of communication and conversation (think dad jokes here!), it seems that every kind of purposeful Body-life speaking, one-to-another, could be placed within this simple structure. This listing is the essence of Paul's simple *diairesis* analysis of Peter's category called "speaking" gifts.

Next, in the same vein, what kind of assistance do people need? Well, everyone needs practical help from time to time. Fixing the washing machine, medical help, childcare, painting the house, etc.

A million ways to help, paid or unpaid. Let's call that serving. People also need emotional help. They need someone to sit and be with them when they are sick or sad, a comforting presence beyond mere words. Or they may need to vent to someone who can really listen more than they give advice. We know the ones who have a comforting grace, like cool water, and we are drawn to them when we are empty. Let's call that showing mercy.

Finally, people need help to move ahead when they run short of resources. These resources could be financial, but they could also come in the form of loaning out a car or giving someone a lawnmower. It could involve fundraising or serving as an advocate for someone or an organization. It includes using connections or expertise on behalf of another. Even more simply, sometimes someone just needs to know that another has done something extraordinary for them (or with them) because they want them to know they are deserving of special love and attention. We need someone who is giving.

Thus, there are three major serving needs: service, showing mercy, and giving, which includes practical, emotional, and resourceful giving. It seems as if every kind of serving can be parceled among those three.

Ta-da! Every speaking and serving need in the Body is covered by these six. Through the inspired genius of *diairesis* analysis, we have arrived! Well . . . almost.

In a group setting, there can be a desperate need for somebody to organize all these servers and speakers. The group needs someone to provide some visible, stand-up-in-front direction—to be the leader. That person has a unique ability to see the whole and its parts, and often seems to have an innate blueprint or organizational chart within themselves. The Greek word for leader, *proistemi*, means "to stand before a group and give direction."[2] We need someone to do the leading, especially when things get dicey.

So through our simple *diairesis* process, looking at the things all people need, we have come up with our own gifting structure. Not mysterious, just practical. If we did not have Paul's categories as a model, we might have come up with others that covered the same ground. But these work so well, so symmetrical . . . as we will now see.

Key 9: The Multicolored Grace of God

So then, that leads us back to the original assertion in Key 1: There Are Seven Gifts. You might ask, "Are there really only seven kinds of people as the *diairesis* consideration seems to indicate?" Both yes and emphatically no. Now it gets interesting.

Peter uses a strange word to describe the *charisma* of God (see 1 Peter 4:10). The word is *poikilos*, which has a basic meaning of "multicolored" or "variegated." The word evokes the idea of stripes or a rainbow of colors. It is often contextually translated as "manifold" or "multifaceted." The image of Peter's term taken in the context of the verse gives an important clue about how the seven kinds of *charisma* are to be viewed and how they practically work.

How many colors are there in the rainbow? If you're geeky, then you will say, "An infinite number." But if you're wanting to simply instruct, you'd say seven. Remember ROY G BIV? Without getting into the complexities of the additive and subtractive color models, Isaac Newton proposed, and others have agreed, that there are seven easily recognized colors in a rainbow, whether seen in the sky or refracted through a prism: red, orange, yellow, green, blue, indigo, and violet. While we can discern a gradient of color within each shade, at some point our eyes tell us that green has become blue, and so on. In that same sense, Paul can be said to be giving us the primary colors of the *charisma* gifts as named points along a continuum of Peter's multicolored (*poikilos*) grace of God.

You can appreciate what Paul has done. As described above, there are a million variations and shades of speaking gifts all covered under the three speaking category headings, and there are another million variations of serving gifts all covered under the three serving category headings. And a million brands of leadership. Seven *charisma* gift category titles cover millions of gift variations. Easy to understand, easy to walk into. Genius. Thanks to Paul and the Holy Spirit's *diairesis* analysis, each of us is named, recognized, covered—and unique. But that's just the start.

The above keys imply several other things about *charisma* gifts. These are important things—even life-changing things. But to help you find your own gifting and the doorway to purpose and connection with God, you'll need a simple tool. Let's move to the application chapter and develop and apply that tool in your life.

Finding My Charisma Gift

In the last chapter, we used the teaching of Peter and Paul to create a set of biblical keys to understand *charisma* gifts. In so doing, we took an important step toward entering into God's purpose for our lives. Recognizing and incorporating these clear and biblical keys should be nonoptional in any definition of spiritual gifts or in developing a tool or application for *charisma* gift determination. These are the keys from the last chapter:

Key 1 There Are Seven Charisma Gifts in Two General Categories

Key 2 We Each Have a Gift

Key 3 Our Gift Is Our General Function in the Body

Key 4 We Have One Charisma Gift

Key 5 We Are Stewards Serving, Not Owners Presiding

Key 6 Our Gift Is Not Our Identity

Key 7 Our Gifts Are Empowered by God

Key 8 There Is a Logical Charisma Gift Structure

Key 9 The Multicolored Grace of God

This chapter will use those keys to create a visual tool that can be used as an effective and easily applied way to begin to zero in on your own *charisma* gifting.

The Pattern of the Charisma Gifts

I remember the day I put up the posters.

I was standing in a large room about to teach a Sunday school class that would be covering the seven *charisma* gifts. I had developed posters derived from a combination of experience and various sources describing characteristics of each of those gifts.* I wanted to put them up around the room so that people could gather and chat under the poster they felt best described them. But in what order? Was "order" even important?

I had been thinking about all the keys described in the previous chapter and how to honor those keys in the arrangement of the posters. I thought of Peter's two categories, Paul's subcategorization into the seven gifts, the many-colored grace of God concept, and the *diairesis* idea that these gifts are God's 360-degree covering of Christ's Body with every need it has.

I wanted to arrange the posters in a way that would be helpful—maybe like the rainbow's colors. So I put the two most basic gifts, the ones that share Peter's category names, on opposite walls—teaching on one wall and serving on the opposite wall. Then I sat and thought, *Now, what goes next to teaching, next to serving, and so on?*

It seemed obvious that the other two speaking gifts—prophecy and exhorting—would be on either side of the more "generic" speaking gift of teaching. And it seemed equally obvious the other two service gifts—mercy and giving—should be on either side of the more "generic" gift of serving. It also seemed that mercy was the

*The posters can be found in Appendix B.

58

natural service partner of exhorting, and teaching was the natural partner of serving. Prophecy and giving were the two things a leader might look to for help and should go on either side of leading. In about ten minutes of stumbling around, a pattern emerged. I didn't really have much time to think more about it as the class members began to stream in.

After a brief explanation, I asked the group to walk around on a "shopping" stroll. I asked them to feel and think, to determine which of the poster descriptions seemed most like them. I cautioned them not to think too hard or to second-guess their decision too much—to ask their mates if they were stuck! I also instructed them that after they decided, they should grab a chair and sit in front of that poster. When everyone found a seat (except a couple of overanalytical engineers), I suggested they interact with questions and topics like these:

- What are a couple of things on the poster that most jumped out to you?
- What do you love about this gift? What scares you?
- Tell a short story about how you and God worked together and used your gift.
- What are some ways others can help you grow in this gift?

Then an amazing thing happened. The murmur of talk slowly grew into a laughing cacophony. Heads nodded, backs were slapped, and fists were bumped all around the room. When the stories began, there were tears and hugs—like finding a lost family. The body posture and facial expressions within each group were eerily similar. And the tone and content of the discussions were different among the groups but similar within each one.

The leaders sat side-by-side, sort of chatting while they scanned the room. The exhorters also surveyed the room but then, apparently satisfied, turned to each other. Ones who served took it upon themselves to hand out blank paper to take notes. One within the gift of giving took pictures of the groups for me, while the teachers corrected my posters. The ones who showed mercy sat face-to-face, ignoring the rest of the activity in the room, deep in eye-to-eye murmured conversation. It was crazy fun!

When it was time to go, most of the people hugged and exchanged phone numbers before they walked out—except the mercy group. They skipped church and stayed talking one-on-one for a much longer time.

The Gift Circle Discussion

From the exercise that day, with feedback on its life-changing impact and subsequent hours of thought and discussion, the application tool that we now call the Gift Circle emerged. A black and white version of the Gift Circle is depicted in the figure. A color version is on the back cover. Starting with the gift of leading and moving clockwise around the circle, the colors follow the ROY G BIV color order: leading-red, prophecy-orange, teaching-yellow, exhorting-green, mercy-blue, serving-indigo, and giving-violet.

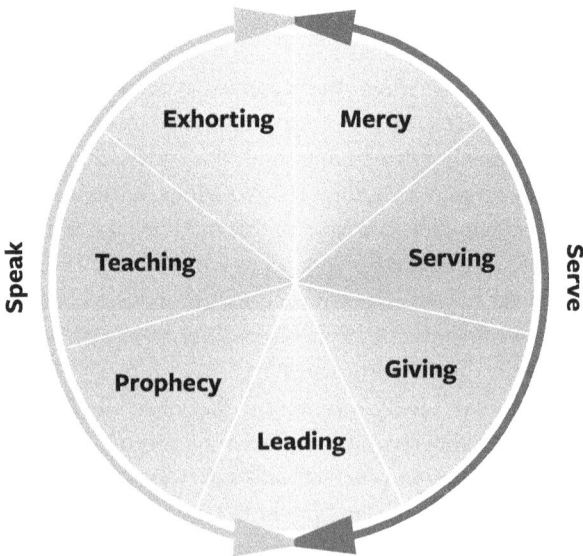

My prophetic friends, of course, give great weight and interesting meaning to the colors, but I'll leave that to you. They did say that no one knows what indigo is, and no one knows what the one serving is actually doing on any given day—a perfect match!

There are several key things to notice about the Circle, many of which were shared by those who have used the tool for me. Let's organize the rest of the discussion into two categories: understanding the layout of the Circle (how to best use it) and having a good initial feel for the definitions of each of the gifts. We'll cover the Gift Circle description and discussion first, and then turn to a more in-depth description of each individual gifting.

Gifts and Personality

Recall the previous discussion about whether gifts are contaminated by personality, if they are essentially the same thing, or if there is some other option. In some sense, it doesn't matter. The outcome for the believer will be the same. A way to look at it is that upon spiritual birth, our spirit is made alive and infused with God. Jesus said that a flow begins from deep within our spirit (conscience, intuition, and communion), flows through our soul (mind, will, and emotions), and is expressed by our body (see John 7:38; 1 Thessalonians 5:23). The spirit is the master, the soul is the steward, and the body is the slave (see Romans 8:14; 1 Corinthians 9:27).

As rivers have different kinds of water, spirits flow with the different flavors of *charisma* that were organized by Paul into seven general categories. That flow is further colored by all the aspects of the soul's characteristics and experiences, both good and bad. Others, upon observing those various tendencies toward behavior, have categorized the observable outflow into personality types, or sometimes better, coping types.

But in any case, I believe that finding your gifting is a combination of grasping what it is and how it works as well as beginning and growing in a partnering relationship with each member of the Trinity. Remember, we aim to work with Him and not just for Him—children far more than employees. As we look to the race we are running and the soul's sanctification, the distinction between spiritual gifts and the soul's part fades (see Hebrews 12:1; 4:10).

No Hard Boundaries between Gifts

In the Gift Circle, the order and placement of the gifts and color scheme isn't random. As explained previously, Peter's two kinds of gifts, teaching and serving, are at the opposite spots of the Circle. There is no top or bottom of the Circle, but I put the leader at the bottom in the "foot-washing" position.

In reference to Peter's "multicolored" comment, I find it interesting that in a rainbow the different visible light colors blend seamlessly into one another around the whole spectrum of light-wave frequencies. Only our human perception draws a sort of boundary line between them. Nature does not.

Many have come to see that the gifts seem to blend into each other as well. There are no hard boundaries. While for the book I have created a gray "rainbow" of pie pieces and placed thin white lines to indicate gift "boundaries," in an actual rainbow, or color circle, there are no actual pie pieces or hard boundaries. They transition from one perceived color to the next along a continuum.*

In the same way, each of the gifts—as we move away from the center of their pie-piece in either direction—begin to blend into the neighboring one. Little by little they shift toward the adjacent hue. At some point, the adjacent gift takes primacy in the blend just as the adjacent color does.

In a way, any one gift is a combination of the two adjacent to it, but with its own unique characteristics. The person who has exhorting as a gift, for example, is part teaching and part mercy but with a uniqueness all his or her own. Even leading is part prophecy (seeing clear direction) and part giving (finding the resources to accomplish a mission) yet is all leading. It is standing before the team and laying out clear direction and order. Each person is obviously one thing (one *charisma*) but from an infinite set. And all

*A color version of this diagram can be found on the back cover.

the colors of light joined together become bright white light—the light of the world!

So if we erase the hard boundaries, recall that the 7 are a 360-degree coverage of the gift needs, and think in terms of Paul naming gifts along the wavelength continuum, another amazing truth about *charisma* emerges.

We Each Occupy an Arc within the Circle

One problem with gift tests and the discussions that follow is the pressure people feel to pick one gift and be that. In years of teaching this topic and helping people discern their gifting, I began to realize another amazing fact about *charisma* gifting: We aren't confined to only one color. In reality, each of us occupies as home base an "arc" within the circle. This arc has most of its length within the focus of one of the gifts, but it may spill into or be strongly "colored" by an adjacent one.

My own arc, for example, is primarily within exhorting, but its end is in teaching; therefore, I am one who exhorts but who's exhortation and encouragement often takes on a teaching (or book writing!) coloring.

A friend of mine leads a business, but his actual energy comes from what that business does. It helps authors and speakers find their message, their voice, and finally, their platform. He comes alive when he sees the excellence he has helped create. His arc? Maybe seventy percent giving and thirty percent leading.

A woman I know well thought her gift was serving because she seemed to always be serving. She would take a whole day and help someone decorate a basement, finish some furniture, put in a flower garden, hang pictures, or create fun projects with her grandchildren. It dawned on my friend, however, that the greatest pleasure she got was in creating something amazing and beautiful and giving it away.

When she looked at the Gift Circle, it appeared that her primary arc was in giving with its tail in serving. That insight began to change how she did things. A growing joy in God-connected intimacy and certainty began to emerge as her giving took on a subtle sense of grace and focus and produced some amazing connections and gifts that were far more than she could have imagined on her own. A sense of guided adventure began to grow within her.

I must repeat that, while the Gift Circle is not specifically in Scripture, every concept that goes into its construction seems to be. Just as the previous chapter discussed that we likely don't have more than one gift, I don't think someone could equally occupy two nonadjacent parts of the circle at once, though I can't be one hundred percent certain about that assertion.

In each case (so far), those who thought they equally occupied both a serving and a speaking gift seemed to always come back and say that the opposite spot was like a "vacation home" but not a suitable permanent habitation. Someone with a speaking gift, for example, takes part in a charitable organization and is faithful to help the needy even though they relish their speaking assignments. Or people with a strong and successful serving gift, perhaps in a growing nonprofit organization, are called to speak to groups about their organization. Because they are mature and fearless, they can speak admirably, but their preference is to always go home to serve. Think of the quote frequently attributed to Mother Teresa: "Spread the love of God through your life but only use words when necessary."

That "visiting" dynamic can be well explained by the next concept.

Speaking and Serving Gifts Motivationally Match

Another pattern within the Gift Circle originated with a friend who clearly saw her gifting was giving, but she stated that she often felt strongly provoked to stir others to join in serving the needs of newly arriving refugees. She wondered if she might have some prophecy in her because she felt strong urges to nudge people; however, she hated speaking in front of people.

As we talked, it became apparent that the serving and speaking gifts mirrored each other across the circle. In some ways, these two giftings meet the same need or accomplish the same thing, but they are differentiated either by serving or speaking as a primary means.

People with the speaking gifts can do so broadly, conceptually, and directionally, while those with serving gifts tend toward focused actions with visibly defined ends and hands-on efforts. Maybe that is why those who have serving gifts tend to outnumber those who have speaking gifts by a good margin. It is not unusual to exhibit a sense of the complementary gifting and even "step across the circle" to bring something about.

Here is a brief description of how the three pairings can be understood:

Giving and Prophecy—These people both see a need, a short-fall, or a misaligned situation and are motivated to see it resolved. The person who gives meets the need through a set of advocacy and resourcing skills. The person who prophesies does so by clearly and articulately pointing out the need and motivating those who have the resources to step up.

Teaching and Serving—The people who have these giftings see practical needs or opportunities for improvement and then move to meet those needs or bring about that improvement. The person teaching prepares instruction to solve the problem or expand the understanding, while the one serving prepares to go and meet the need personally or with a team.

Exhorting and Mercy—These two giftings are motivated by comfort and courage. The person exhorting, especially if in a leadership position, may motivate others toward all sorts of encouraging goals and objectives, while the one showing mercy may quietly seek to bring personal one-on-one comfort, encouragement, and joy through his or her presence and his or her carefully chosen words of healing and restoration.

People with the gift of leading span the gap, providing both service and speaking when needed, but they will quickly work themselves out of a nonleadership role by finding a speaker or server who is better suited to fill the need.

Charisma Gift Synopsis

The second important topic necessary for effective Gift Circle application is for you to be provided more than a one-line summary of each of the seven *charisma* gifts. These one paragraph summaries are derived from many sources and people. Each description has a tagline that attempts to summarize their primary motivation and a description of how the gift might change as its arc approaches the boundary on either side. There is a much more detailed description of each *charisma* gift in Appendix B.

Some of these descriptions describe the in-Church or Body-life objectives of each gifting rather than its similar, though differently expressed, gifting applied in the world in day-to-day and professional life. But I want to stress that each gift has direct application everywhere. Only the language and approach will change to fit the situation. Probably over 95 percent of all gifting applications are not within the church walls. You cannot not be you! And you don't spend that much time in church.

For example, I spent much of my focus on Christian-related ventures. Yet in my life as an exhorter-teacher and an engineer, I gravitated away from sitting in an office doing design calculations in favor of working with local governments, "exhorting" and "teaching" them how to bring about changes to improve the water quality and natural green beauty. As I think back over those times, great and clear Father-God intervention came out of my mostly unwitting application of my gifting in that municipal government realm.

In another example, I have a friend whose gifting is leading/giving. She started a very successful cleaning business and then used the profits to outfit vans with washing machines and driers, parking them near homeless campsites and offering free clothes washing, coffee, and friendship.

All of life is holy. All of who you are is a child of God—even the career parts. Maybe especially those!

Here, then, are paragraph-long descriptions of each of the seven *charisma* gifts listed in Romans 12.

Leading—*eliminating group dysfunction and bringing vision and order*

The one who leads, as its Greek word *proistemi* (which means "to stand before") shows, is born to be in front of, to preside (not rule) over people, and to influence vision and direction. Those leading can often see the end from the beginning and most of the steps in between. They have an inner sense of what needs to become and to be done, and how God might be organizing groups of people to do so. They have a knack for calling attention to key directions or important issues, applying both pressure and wisdom to change things. They recognize gifts and talents and rally others to a cause or vision. Their names are often at the top of the bulletin or company organization chart, though they often wisely prefer a less visible role. They thrive under pressure and value loyalty. They can temporarily step into any of the gifts until they find someone able to fill that role.

On the counterclockwise giving side, those who have a leading gift can tend toward charitable organizations and causes. On the clockwise prophecy side, those who have a leading gift lean toward strong speaking roles and calling an organization to right-action in society.

Prophecy—*eliminating what is wrong and bringing what is right*

People with the prophecy gifting call the Church to become what God is calling it to be. The one who prophesies can often seem to sense something that is morally wrong, unjust, or inappropriate long before others. They often tend to see things in black and white or see the black and white parts of things. They communicate and enforce revealed truth. This term can be confusing because the term, differently applied but related, shows up in all three components of Paul's structure. When mature, those who have the prophetic gifting are loyal advisors who can seemingly see "over the horizon."

On the counterclockwise leading side, those with the prophecy gifting tend to lead or be part of a leadership team, helping to bring God's intent and design to an organization or to an individual's life. Their focus tends to be on what needs improvement or is falling short of vision. On the clockwise teaching side, they can tend to look at what can be improved or changed and use scriptural principles and approaches to do so. Those who have the prophecy gifting can sometimes seem to project criticism. It might be that no matter how careful they are, someone will feel criticized. But at their mature best, they can lovingly help the Body of Christ to "shape up."

Teaching—eliminating what is ignorant or false and bringing vital, living truth

The one who teaches is concerned with truth from God and His Word and communicating it to both the Body and to individuals. Those with the teaching gift are more about true and false than the right and wrong of prophets. They tend to be aroused by poor or misleading teaching or ignorance of biblical concepts and precepts and have a deep appreciation for truth well spoken. They are sensitive to mixture, exaggeration, and inaccuracies that, in their view, may warp truth and distort God's character and His Word. They are encouraged by people who are filled with an understanding of and appreciation for God's Word.

On the counterclockwise prophecy side, they will tend toward seeing false or incomplete teaching as wrong and needing correction. On the clockwise exhorting side, they become more and more focused on encouraging people to use biblical truth in specific ways.

Exhorting—eliminating wounding and confusion and bringing healing and purpose

The word used for "exhorting" in Romans 12 is *parakaleo*, which, in its noun form, is used multiple times by Jesus in John's gospel as a descriptive name for the Holy Spirit (see John 14:16, 26; 15:26; 16:7). Its meaning is complex and includes consoling, encouraging, representing, helping, carrying, and more. This Greek word was also a term used when someone was running a marathon. Near the end of the race when the runner was exhausted, the designated *paraclete* was allowed to run alongside and call out encouragement—thus its meaning "alongside to call." The one who exhorts is concerned about whether individuals and institutions are joyfully growing well into all they are purposed by God to be. They are aroused by stuck and wounded people and are encouraged by people who are moving in the strength of their gifting and calling. They are filled with projects and vision. They tend to be good at seeing into people's hearts and situations effectively. They are generally good communicators.

On the counterclockwise teaching side, people with the exhorting gifting will lean toward teaching that is organized, practically applied, and encouraging. On the clockwise mercy side, exhorters lean toward bringing inner healing, teaching others how to practically help people, and more. An exhorter's goal is not healing or freeing for its own sake only, but also for the sake of the fulfillment of the destiny calling within the person.

Giving—eliminating lack and investing in high quality gain

The Greek word for this gift is *metadidomi*, which means not simply to give, but "to give with a specific end purpose in mind; to impart or bestow." The person gifted in giving sees what others are meant to accomplish and finds ways and means to help them. They have a unique ability and favor to see how God might be providing, and they are trusted with resources to help bring that about. They typically shun publicity but know how to use it to accomplish a project. They are thrifty and want organizations to be excellent in managing resources. Maybe most importantly, the most mature give in nonfinancial ways through advocacy, connections, and assistance at just the right time—reflecting the Father's *energema* aid.

On the counterclockwise serving side, people with giving giftings lean toward practical ways of bringing excellent resources and special beauty or a distinct quality to an event or initiative. On the clockwise leading side, they lean toward larger efforts designed to efficiently undergird high quality causes and organizations.

Serving—eliminating physical needs and focusing on "get-er-done"

The word for serving, *diakonia*, is widely used for the act of serving or ministering to another. While (as we will see in the next chapter) everyone has an assigned ministry/job (*diakonia*) from Jesus, people who have a serving gifting are specifically suited to seeing and solving practical needs. They move, often individually, to make that happen. They show up with food, vacuum the house, and take out the trash. They value practical actions that fix problems, things, and situations. They often have trucks, trailers, and tools. They typically shun publicity and organizational entanglements if it slows down the work of serving.

On the counterclockwise mercy side, those with a serving gifting can express deep compassion and then move practically to fix things. They weep with the weeping and then roll up their sleeves. On the clockwise giving side, serving people begin to show a stronger drive to solve more complex problems or more foundational causes below the surface of the physical need and lack of resources.

Mercy—eliminating pain and investing in joy

People showing a mercy gifting have a keen and sometimes amazing ability to sense people's feelings and emotional conditions. They are aroused to action when they see someone in pain or lacking joy. They often seem to be able to sense things that are emotionally off or inauthentic. They can easily connect deeply and are a salve to the soul. They may not be the first to the hospital, but they are often the last to leave—with the patient.

On the counterclockwise exhorting side, people with a mercy gifting may take on a bit of instruction or advice giving, but in a very loving and concerned way. On the clockwise serving side, the mercy gifted folks often give practical advice and help make necessary changes happen.

Finding My Gifting

So . . . finally! Let's demystify finding your arc in the circle—your *charisma* gifting. Here are a few key things to know.

Finding through Connection

First, remember the "one thing" from chapter 2: the Trinity does everything with us. *Charisma* gift identification and refinement comes with God-connected experience—not simply studying or taking a test, though tests or another stepwise approach can be helpful. Our gift comes to light as we go about doing things with Him—and not related to church only. The Holy Spirit is vested in us understanding our gifting, and He is called the Helper or Advocate who demonstrates many roles, including comfort, conviction of sin, guidance, teaching, direction, bringing to remembrance, empowering, and more. And sort of like tuning a guitar, as we begin to better understand and take on the works God has prepared for us, the sense of connection and empowerment increases.

Uncertainty

Second, there will be uncertainty—that is human! In Key #7 we discussed learning how to honor the flow of the Holy Spirit from within us. It is not difficult. In fact, we were made to do so, even with that uncertainty. Knowing and moving in our gifting takes patience. There will be trial, error, and success, as well as a growing inner joy at accomplishment. In Acts 15, the biggest decision of the early Church, grace versus law, was to be made and all the greats were gathered seeking God. Their response written to the Gentile believers is very telling: "It seemed good to the Holy Spirit and to us" (Acts 15:28). Seemed good!? They were open to anything God wanted. They felt led, and they trusted God to handle things. That is good enough. There are checks and balances, of course, and any book on the subject will enumerate them; however, it is not about technique but relationship. There will almost always be some uncertainty in this way of living, but there will never be risk. I am uncertain if this is the perfect decision, but I am certain of the Holy Spirit who cares for me. I'm good.

Basic How-To

I have developed a simple three-step exercise that has proven very effective in helping individuals zero in on their *charisma* arc in the Gift Circle.

Initially, it is fairly easy to get a good idea of your gifting since there are only two major "functional" gift types—speaking and serving. Most know which of those two is most attractive right away. Within those two, there are only seven basic gifts. Even through simply looking at the descriptions above, I have found it has been common to zero in on the general area of attraction or maybe even get a sense of your "arc." So many in class have said, "Yes, sir. That one is me to a tee," often with smiling spouses or friends.

Zeroing in on that gifting is somewhat different for older and younger people. Older people, in their forties and up, tend to have had a longer and wider experience of career and interpersonal accomplishments in and out of church circles. On the negative side, they may have settled into some habits and thought patterns that are counterproductive. And on the positive side, they probably have had a lot of life and ministry experiences to peer through to try to see their primary motivation. In any case, the diversity of that history can make finding their *charisma* gifting a bit harder. They may think, "I could do any of these things." A 92-year-old patriarch pastor friend commented to me that the older he gets, the more toward the center of the circle he feels that he moves, and the easier it is to "visit" another spot if a need arises. That might be true.

With younger people, review of the descriptions and a few questions typically will point them in the right starting direction. I have watched young people respond to the questions below. There is often a good bit of nodding and head scratching. It is good to see the lights turn on after the confusion about gift structure is cleared up. "You mean I'm not a tongue in the Body?"

No matter your age, I'm inviting you to the same simple exercise to clear up potential questions you might have about your gifting. Pay attention to your initial, intuitive impressions and feelings more than your mental analysis. Here we go!

The Three Steps

● **Step 1—Is my primary gift area speaking or serving?**

Imagine yourself in the following circumstance as you monitor your feelings and inner voice. Someone comes to you and asks, "Hey, I was wondering if you'd be willing to give a twenty-minute speech on some topic of interest to you at the City Council meeting this Friday. I know it is Wednesday, but the other speaker cancelled. They try to have a local person give an interesting talk once a quarter. Maybe one hundred people will be there—probably the mayor, too. Oh, it will be televised."

Okay. What are you feeling? Are you excited but nervous thinking, "I might could do that—maybe." Or are you legitimately mortified and terrified at how bad you'd most probably do? You and others know speaking is not your strong suit.

If you felt nervously excited even though a bit afraid, odds are good you should start looking for your gifting in the speaking area. Go to Step 2.

If you are mortified and know that is absolutely *not* you (and your friends gently agree), then the serving gift area seems your best bet for first focus. This does not mean you cannot speak in front of people (remember Mother Teresa), just that it is not your primary mode. Skim Step 2 and go to Step 3.

● **Step 2—If my primary gift is speaking, which of the three might it be?**

If you were given one chance to speak to your church on a Sunday morning, or to a group or company, would your focus or motivation tend to be centered more in approach A, B, or C below? What emotion, motivation, and direction seems to outweigh any other?

A. You are complimentary to them, but also feel an itch toward being gently corrective to help them be the best they can be ("I think we're missing something here!"). Perhaps it is about a great opportunity they could, or should, be doing something about or doing better in. It might feel as if you are bringing up something that needs to be improved or redirected—maybe bringing up a need they might be overlooking.

B. You are excited to tell them about an amazing truth you found in Scripture that had an impact on your life ("I just have to show you this pattern in Romans that is so interesting and applicable to us."). Maybe it is something you found that they might find exciting or transformative. For a work group, it might mean sharing some pertinent company improvement training that you have found to be applicable or informational to them in a way that you hope will be insightful and helpful. You are bringing important information.

C. You seem to have a clear vision about the strengths and calling of the church or group, and you want to encourage them about their amazing abilities or history ("You guys are amazing and I'm going to tell you all about it!"). You encourage them when you speak about God's love, provision, and protection. You might share specifically how they can walk more fully in that. Or for an organization, you encourage them regarding the strengths and possibilities within the firm or organization. You describe a realistically great path forward and urge them to be their best selves and go for it. You are encouraging and exhorting.

The first (A) would point toward a prophecy gifting—seeing a correction or a shortfall that you have trouble simply ignoring. The second (B) would indicate a teaching gifting—being excited to illustrate and apply biblical truth or important new information. And the third (C) would indicate an exhorting gifting—being excited about what God has put inside of someone or an organization.

Moving forward from this exercise, begin to pay attention to your inner motivation in various situations, and let it seep into you over the next several months. Review the Gift Circle with an arc in mind that has its main part in that gift area. Would it edge into an adjacent one as well? Ask God for insight. Sometimes, without being critical, you can ask yourself how you would have preached the last Sunday sermon a bit differently and why. Then begin to patiently look for God-given opportunities to help, assist, step in, etc., in speaking roles. The timing is in God's hands. We can slow Him down far more than we can speed Him up. But running ahead of Him is to court disaster. "Wait on the Lord" is everywhere in Scripture (see Isaiah 40:28–31; Psalm 27:14; 37:7; 130:5).

● Step 3—What is my serving motivation?

If speaking is probably not your *charisma* area, then envision this situation. Read slowly. See this scenario in your mind's eye.*

You are a uniformed server in a fancy restaurant that has a big table of businesspeople celebrating a corporate year-end success. You and several others are handling that table. The restaurant is busy, drinks are very late, and the table is growing restless and impatient. A young server on your team finally emerges from the kitchen with a tray loaded with long-overdue fancy drink orders. But the server forgets there is a step down to the table and slips slightly, and the tray becomes unbalanced, tilts, and spills all the drinks on the floor with a crash, a splash, and a clatter. It all seems to happen in slow motion as you freeze in horrified shock. The restaurant hushes. The table looks on with impatient disgust. You are standing there. Close your eyes and imagine that situation, see it, and feel it.

Here is the question: Without overthinking, what do you feel an immediate urge to do? You feel you must . . .

- Go straight to the mess ("It's a *mess!*"), urgently needing to get things orderly and cleaned up before somebody steps on the glass or slips on the splattered puddle.
- Go straight to the person ("Oh, my poor friend!), bringing comforting words to defuse the embarrassment they surely

---

*I believe a story somewhat similar to this was first introduced by the Institute in Basic Life Principles many years ago.

feel and offering your emotional support in whatever they most need.

- Go straight to the kitchen ("They need drinks, and fast!") to get new drink orders going, knowing the table is waiting impatiently and feeling a need to serve the clients, meet the need for drinks, and cover the restaurant's reputation.

The desperate need to clean up the mess would point toward *service*. The sudden strong concern for your fellow server would indicate *mercy*. And the need to get those amazing drinks (probably comped) to the people who ordered them would indicate *giving*.

As with the speaking gifts, it would be good to think about this scenario, pay attention to your inner motivation in various situations, and let it seep into you over the next months. Review the Gift Circle and descriptions, with an arc in mind, and consider whether an adjacent gifting seems pertinent. Ask God for insight. Pay attention to nudges and simple one-shot opportunities to step in and let your gifting flow.

- The leader ("Somebody needs to organize all this!")—if all you want to do is to step in and shout orders to the slow and confused wait staff or, more calmly, you think about all the speaking or serving responses above and say to yourself, "Well, I could really do any of those. But if the organization is inefficient and ineffective, then these things are of secondary importance," then you might be "one who leads" with diligence. That is their classic response.

Okay. How are you feeling? Remember that our knowledge of our gifting area comes with connected experience (trial and error and success), not simply studying or taking a test, and a growing inner joy at the connection and growing lifestyle change. And patience. Remember, too, as Jesus noted, to avoid self-promotion and rather to be faithful in little things, hidden things, financial things, and things that help promote another's life. Then Jesus will bring about your promotion in fulfilling and stable ways. As mentioned, the point is to do our best to listen to God and follow His lead, not simply to identify our gifting.

Testimonies and Stories

Recently as I have had conversations with three different men, their career frustrations or opportunities came up. In each case, the man had some sense of "missing some church thing" by being so involved in his profession.

In one situation, the man had just been hired to guide the transition of a medical research company into the production and fielding of a groundbreaking and money-saving medical instrument. We did an abbreviated three-step "gift finding" conversation, which took two minutes. He saw the new job as a promotion from God, as a next assignment using his leadership (with an arc into giving) gifting. He knew that he was being entrusted to bring a group and an important medical breakthrough to the world as his new Jesus-given ministry (*diakonia*). He saw that his role was far beyond simple management, but he was to bring life and purpose to the organization. He dropped his fork, misted up, and his hands shook with excitement. Right then he knew he was at the very center of God's will for his life.

In another case, a man was collapsing under the stress of providing financial advice to a set of clients that was too big. Yet, he felt driven to maximize his income. So he kept going. As we spoke, he began to get a sense of his gifting almost completely as one who gives. He realized that he had much more to give than financial advice. He agreed to pray to ask God who should be his focus, even his "flock" to serve. When he saw this assignment as his gift and calling in the Body and as outreach, his whole posture changed. He began to more joyfully check off each of the next steps he was going to take. New insight brings new vision. I checked in weeks later, and he was all smiles. The going got way more peaceful.

Another man was a pastor of a large church in the southwest. He shared that he had taught the Enneagram, and he felt both elated at the interest and deflated, feeling the Enneagram tells people who they are but not what they are made to do. It didn't help people figure out their purpose. I asked him about spiritual gifts, and he expressed incredulity at the mushiness of that topic in his circle. He believed it would get no traction. He stated, "Everybody tried some sort of gift test, and everybody moved on, some keeping the answer somewhere in the back of their mind." It was a bust. After I led him into a realization of his own *charisma* arc (exhorting with a strong mercy piece) and I discussed those implications in his current ministry, he asked to see the "Gift Circle thing." Three days later, he called to talk. Four days after that, he asked for help in constructing a teaching for his church. He was hooked.

Earlier in the book, I mentioned that I had talked with nursing students. They were asked to describe their experience with the three steps. Here are a few:

"I believe I occupy the serving aspect of this arc, slightly in the mercy wedge. I can see a few examples of this in my life. In one of my old jobs, I would often bring patients to their cars after they were discharged from the hospital. I had one instance where the patient was completely lost and turned around in the hospital. I ended up pushing her around for half an hour."

"I have been born and raised Pentecostal (Assembly of God). Prior to the lecture, I knew exactly what the subject of 'gifts' was. Over the years, I have done many different questionnaires to see what my top gifts were. This demonstration with just a few easy questions made it so simple. The *charisma* that feels most like me is showing mercy. Showing mercy to me means forgiving others quickly when something goes wrong. It means loving others even when you may not want to."

"The most interesting thing about Andy's lecture to me was actually getting to answer the questions about our own spiritual gift. Instead of just learning about the gifts, I was able to relate them to myself, which was very interesting. I also liked how we looked at all the gifts because I was able to relate to some of the others and create an 'arc.'"

In Summary

I must repeat, the Gift Circle is not in the Bible, per se, but each of the biblical keys in chapter 3 is tacitly or explicitly incorporated in its design. It is sort of a combined visualization and application of all those truths. It has since proven to be incredibly helpful in explaining the wisdom of God's seven-fold listing, showing which gifts seemingly blend into which other gifts, and finding our gifting arc.

I also need to state that Paul goes on to give a set of warnings about the use of gifts. While important to understand, that discussion would extend this chapter in a whole new direction. I have placed them in Appendix C and encourage the interested reader to look carefully there.

So . . . we have a "function." We are a body part. We have one *charisma* gift focus that moves along an arc for life. And we depend on each other. Got it?

The Diagram Continued

In the diagram below you can see that Paul's analysis fits a particular *diairesis* pattern that we are in the process of uncovering. We are now ready to add the first Level 3 category—the *charisma* gift list enumerating the primary colors of the various functions lived in partnership with Holy Spirit.

Now we are standing at the entrance to purpose. Okay. Let's find out how we use our gifting in the next chapter as we find our "career."

The Spiritual Gifts Blueprint

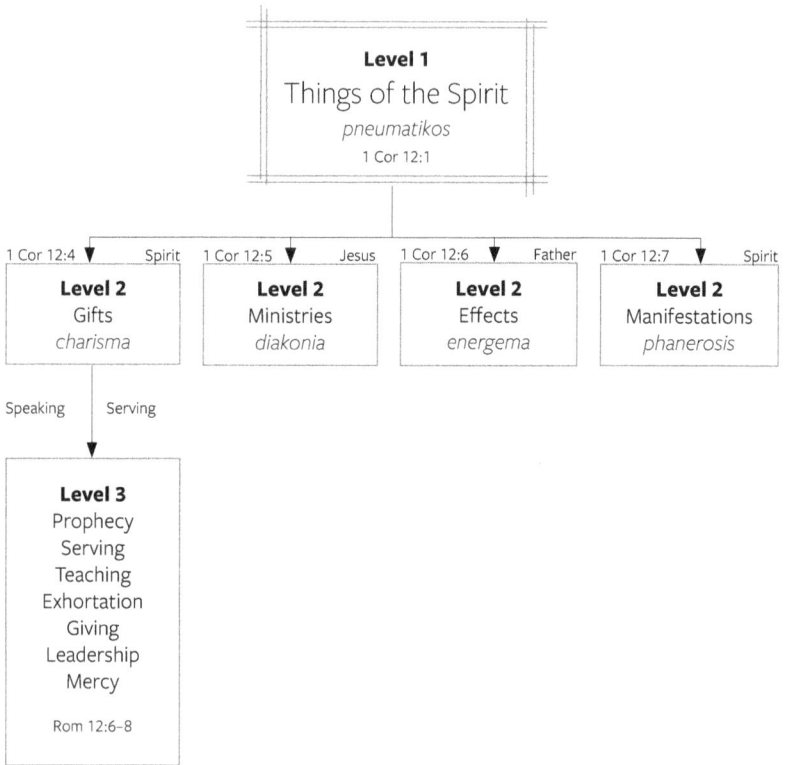

```
┌─────────────────────────────────┐
│           Level 1               │
│     Things of the Spirit        │
│         pneumatikos             │
│          1 Cor 12:1             │
└─────────────────────────────────┘
```

1 Cor 12:4 ▼ Spirit	1 Cor 12:5 ▼ Jesus	1 Cor 12:6 ▼ Father	1 Cor 12:7 ▼ Spirit
Level 2 Gifts *charisma*	**Level 2** Ministries *diakonia*	**Level 2** Effects *energema*	**Level 2** Manifestations *phanerosis*

Speaking | Serving

```
┌─────────────────────────────────┐
│           Level 3               │
│           Prophecy              │
│           Serving               │
│           Teaching              │
│          Exhortation            │
│            Giving               │
│          Leadership             │
│            Mercy                │
│                                 │
│          Rom 12:6–8             │
└─────────────────────────────────┘
```

5

Jesus and Ministry

The Move

I remember the day we made the decision. My wife and I were living comfortably in the deep South. We had steady jobs, close friends, a cute little house, a new baby—all fine. But when we spoke about our lives, we agreed that something was not quite right. Though we could not have defined things very well back then, we knew that we had begun to feel a bit adrift without sail or wind. Any forward movement involved steady paddling. We did volunteer work with inner-city children, and I liked my job just fine, even though I knew it was not the best long-term fit. While these things worked in the foreground of our lives, we had some inner sense of purpose that began aching in the background. We both knew and had experienced God-ordained periods of waiting—but it didn't seem to be like that, either. It felt more like a whining car engine ready for a shift.

On visits to family in Nashville, we became attracted to a church and a spiritual movement. We found that we came more alive when we were there. So on the inside, we said a subtle yes. And taking a deep breath, we decided to pull the trigger. No job, no house, no friends, but we had a sense of excitement and some hidden reason beyond reason. We later agreed it was the best and hardest decision we ever made. I justified it to myself by saying, "We're going to have another child. Who could turn down having grandparents and free babysitting available?"

In retrospect, it is clear that the gentle nudge of Jesus was an opportunity to move to another assignment in His Kingdom. And if we sought that Kingdom first, then everything else would find its place (see Matthew 6:33). On the career side, my engineering consulting seemed to take on a life of its own as my reputation in a fast-expanding field grew to national prominence. Oh, the God stories! On the Kingdom side, relationships happened, insights and ideas flowed, and we began to feel traction. There were lots of mistakes and dark opposition as well. Perfect! If you meet Satan head on, you know you're going in the right direction.

Many of my Christian friends who have a similar heart for listening and following as best they can also tell similar stories. Some have notable public lives—a well-known musician, a governor, a music producer. Another started a private Christian school that now has 350 students, and another unlikely middle-aged heroine started a nonprofit that rescues sex trafficking slaves. She even spoke on the TED Talk stage about going on sting operations with the FBI! Many others, like myself, have lives that seem less outwardly visible or successful, but that is only because of how *we* sometimes define visibility and success—not how God does.

I want to emphasize that every story and every path is different. Yours is unique to you. In God's family, like any great family, each one is treated a bit like an only child in the eyes of the loving parents. So be you—proudly. Enjoy your walk, encourage another's, and hold God's hand. Be brave. Be okay with uncertainty and mistakes, lots of mistakes. Be excellent and faithful in little things. And you'll sense and hear, "Well done, good and faithful servant! You have been faithful with a few things; I will put you in charge of many things. Come and share your master's happiness" (Matthew 25:23 NIV).

That is what this chapter is all about.

Ministry (Diakonia) Overview

Recall that the focus of this book is discussing God's unique four-part grace package described in 1 Corinthians 12:1–11: gifts (*charisma*), ministries (*diakonia*), effects (*energema*), and manifestations (*phanerosis*). In the last two chapters, we looked at *charisma* gifts—the seven basic motivational types, lenses, or primary colors: teaching, exhorting, prophecy, leading, serving, showing mercy, and giving. We saw that this list, given by inspiration to Paul, provides an infinite variety that is encapsulated in seven basic type headings—each one with an inner draw toward an inherent God-given and God-empowered ability. These abilities, with others, cover the basic needs of people both in the Body of Christ and outside. You are gifted.

In this chapter and the next, we will focus on the second part of that four-legged package: What is my job and my career? Recall that in 1 Corinthians 12:5 Paul says, "There are varieties [*diairesis*] of ministries [*diakonia*], and the same Lord." The Greek word *diakonia* has a history with many related meanings all having to do with some type of advice, service, or assistance. Both lawyers and housecleaners provide *diakonia*. The word "deacon" comes from the same root as *diakonia* and refers to those appointed, or simply recognized by friends, who provide special assistance in a Body of Christ setting (see Acts 6:3 or 1 Timothy 3:8–10).

In our broader context, the word *diakonia* is used by Paul in 1 Corinthians 12 to define someone's current Jesus-given, Kingdom-related role—and secondarily, their longer-term career path. For many people, the center of their *diakonia* is outside the church walls where people least expect to encounter Jesus but where they likely need Him most.

Your Kingdom career path will change and mature over time—as will you. And at some point, a growing sense of a plan, purpose, and vision will emerge and mature. Understanding that this dynamic is real, is God-given, and is actually happening is important. In God's eyes, it is not a random walk. It is purposeful and planned.

And just like the understanding and use of our *charisma* gifting is done in connection with the Holy Spirit, the way *diakonia* is best perceived and then joyfully carried out is in intimate connection with Jesus. Interested? Okay! Let's go!

Paul's Diairesis Analysis of Ministry (Diakonia)

In the same way that Paul lists and explains the *charisma* part of God's grace package (see Romans 12), in Ephesians 4, he gives us both the context and details of the *diakonia* part. I have skipped a few verses that are not directly pertinent to our discussion and ensured the same words are translated identically. Read it slowly and carefully—it is stuffed with patterns of meaning.

> [1]I . . . urge you to walk in a manner worthy of the calling with which you have been called, [2]with all humility and gentleness, with patience, bearing with one another in love, [3]being diligent to keep [*tereo*] the unity [*henotes*] of the Spirit in the bond of peace. [4]There is one body and one Spirit, just as you also were called in one hope of your calling; [5]one Lord, one faith, one baptism, [6]one God and Father of all who is over all and through all and in all. [7]But to each one of us grace [*charis*] was given according to the measure [*metron*] of Christ's gift [*dòrea*]. [8]Therefore it says, "When He ascended on high . . . and He gave gifts [*doma*] to people." . . . [11]And He gave some as apostles, some as prophets, some as evangelists, some as pastors and teachers, [12]for the equipping of the saints for the work of ministry [*diakonia*], for the building up of the body of Christ; [13]until we all attain [*katantaó*] to the unity [*henotes*] of the faith, and of the knowledge of the Son of God, to a mature man, to the measure [*metron*] of the stature which belongs to the fullness of Christ. [14]As a result, we are no longer to be children . . . [15]but speaking the truth in love [*agape*], we are to grow up in all aspects into Him who is the head, that is, Christ, [16]from whom the whole body, being fitted and held together by what every supporting ligament supplies, according to the proper working [*metron*] of each individual part, causes the growth of the body for the building up of itself in love [*agape*].
>
> Ephesians 4:1–8, 11–16

As in our discussion of the keys to understanding *charisma* gifts in chapter 3, let's make note of five key *diakonia* ministry concepts described here by Paul. Note that while the *charisma* keys refer primarily to the Holy Spirit and the individual, the *diakonia* keys refer primarily to Christ and His Body expressed through its relationships and roles—your relationships and roles.

Key 1: The Two Unities

In Jesus' final prayer, He prays specifically that we would all be one with the Trinity and with each other (see John 17:20–23). Jesus refers to two unities: united with God and united with each other. In Ephesians 4, Paul explains exactly how, through *diakonia*, these two unities come about. And understanding and working within these unities is our first key.

The first unity is a gift to the Body. We are to be "diligent to keep [maintain] the unity of the Spirit in the bond of peace" (Ephesians 4:3). That unity is provided to the Body, and it is one that we are to work diligently to treasure and preserve. In verses 5 and 6, Paul emphasizes the facts and facets of this given unity saying there is one Body, Spirit, hope, Lord, faith, baptism, and God. It is clear that these things are defined and provided by God to His one Body. No divisions. No splits. Appreciate diversity. Work diligently at unity, as it is not an option for a healthy Body. Period.

The second unity is one to be attained, not just maintained. We maintain the first unity "until we all attain to the unity of" (the second unity, verse 13). Paul then describes what that second attained unity consists of. It is faith, knowledge of Christ Jesus, and a mature stature belonging to the fullness of Christ. Together we become Christian "grown-ups." It is something we all work to grow up into, or else it cannot be called unity.

Christ's passionate will is that we understand, appreciate, and maintain the first unity while we work together to attain the second. We are to work together to build each other up, hold each other up, and lift each other up. We, together, are immature in stature, but are growing into that maturity that looks like the fullness of Christ.

But here is the problem. We, like the Ephesians here, are mostly ignorant of this whole idea. We have often failed to recognize the given unity, and we have not worked to maintain it. We have not found ways to appreciate or even accommodate a truth that shades differently from our own. We have criticized the immaturity in another while overlooking our own. Such comparative and competitive attitudes make it hard to attain to the second unity.

When we (mostly out of ignorance that these unities are a thing) act this way, bad things happen—and they certainly have happened. Look at our track record. There are currently an estimated 45,000 denominations worldwide and probably many thousand other separate expressions.[1]

But Christ seems to continue to work in local bodies and across cities and nations to help us grow to appreciate and be curious about differences without prematurely judging others. And we are encouraged to allow others to help grow us up into the "you" of the chapter's introduction.

How does this happen? That is the next key.

Key 2: The Gift of Christ

In Ephesians 4:7–8, 11 (given above), many translations use the word "gift" or "gave." And since it is translated that way, many have simply equated Paul's subsequent discussion as another discussion of spiritual gifts. But what Paul is actually discussing is something quite different from *charisma*. The word "gift" in verse 7 is not the word *charisma* but the word *dòrea*. It is called an "epexegetic genitive," which is a technical way of saying that the phrase literally means the "gift consisting of Christ." He gave of Himself. In verses 8 and 11, the words for "gift" and "gave" are generic words for a present and putting in place. None are *charisma*.

What Paul is saying in this passage is that Christ gave of Himself to the Body. He is the gift. Not some external thing, not some grace package, not some talent, but He, Himself. It is your measure of Christ (see next key) and not in terms of quantity ("I've got a half gallon of Christ!") but in terms of specific, Christ-connected maturing ability to carry out your Christ-planned assignment at the real-time direction of Christ within you.

Throughout this passage, Paul is using both an organizational and physical body metaphor for the Church. In verse 15, he calls Christ the "head" of the body, and is not only referring to an organizational leader, but to the head's physical essence, the brain, within and directing the body.

We gain insight when we think of Jesus as the body's "brain" as much as the organization's head. The brain's function is, in more than a hundred billion ways, to communicate with, influence, and control the body. Every sense organ and cell receives instructions and support from the brain. Every body system is coordinated by the brain, and the body itself moves by the brain's instruction and motivation. That is how the human body, and the Body of Christ, functions. "He put all things in subjection under His feet, and made Him head over all things to the church, which is His body, the fullness of Him who fills all in all" (Ephesians 1:22–23).

This connection to Christ flows primarily from within us where Christ dwells, with clear guidance and clarity from Scripture. Scripture tells *us* how to operate—Jesus tells *you* how to operate.

You are generally qualified by your *charisma*, but the presence and work of Christ within and through you makes you specifically qualified and skilled for a particular assignment and career. This principle is what Paul is writing about when he says, "There are varieties of ministries, and the same Lord" in 1 Corinthians 12. Connection to Christ is key. Christ in me, the hope of glory—and in fulfilling employment (see Colossians 1:27).

How does this connection happen?

Key 3: The Measure of Christ

Paul uses a strange word, *metron*, three times in these verses. And getting what he means is revolutionary in understanding *diakonia*. Many translations inadvertently obscure this pattern by translating this same word several different ways in these passages. Let's undo that and look at verses 7, 13, and 16. (I have inserted the word *metron* where it goes in each verse.) What is Paul saying?

But to each one of us grace was given according to the **measure** [*metron*] of Christ's gift.

Ephesians 4:7

Jesus measured an aspect of Himself out to each person—the gift (*dòrea*) of Christ. That measure, that *diakonia* grace, defines and empowers my unique assignment, my job, within the Body of Christ—ever-changing and maturing as I make use of my basic *charisma* gift, faithfully and excellently doing the thing that seems set before me.

From whom the whole body, being fitted and held together by what every joint supplies, according to the proper working within **measure** [*metron*] of each individual part, causes the growth of the body for the building up of itself in love.

Ephesians 4:16

Each person is to work without jealousy or comparison within their allotted measure. God never compares us to another—only to His plan and desire for each of us. Remember the story of curious (or maybe jealous) Peter asking Jesus, "What about John?" Jesus responds, "What is that to you? You follow Me!" (John 21:21–22).

The parables of Jesus begin to take on new meaning within this context. He is the head of the Body and tells us His expectations. The parables of the talents and the minas (see Matthew 25:14–30; Luke 19:11–27) reveal His displeasure with our doing nothing with what we have been given, no matter the size of His measure in our lives. I am to focus on my measure, creating excellence in my assigned place in connection with Jesus and others. That is my job. And these jobs change, grow, and mature as we demonstrate faithful excellence.

When we each choose to be faithful, however imperfectly, an amazing thing happens.

Until we all attain to the unity of the faith, and of the knowledge of the Son of God, to a mature man, to the **measure** [*metron*] of the stature which belongs to the fullness of Christ.

Ephesians 4:13

As each does his or her part, the inevitable outcome is that the Body assembled measures up to the fullness of the stature of Christ. My local expression of the Body looks, acts, and has an impact on the world as Jesus would—with some assembly required! Why? Because it is Jesus that is measured out and works within each one of us. In verse 15, Paul says the outcome is that we grow up in all aspects into Him who is the head in all aspects—yours and mine. We. Grow. Up.

But we need human guidance to do so. So . . .

Key 4: The Equippers

Paul states that a special aspect of Christ giving of Himself is that He assigns trusted individuals in every local expression of His Body to job descriptions that indicate special equipping roles: apostle, prophet, evangelist, pastor, and teacher (see verse 11). These people work "for the building up of the body of Christ"* (verse 12). These five are titles for *diakonia* ministries (not *charisma* gifts). Paul, for example, was probably gifted (*charisma*) as one who exhorts (see Acts 20:1-2), and his eventual ministry (*diakonia*) was as an apostle. But he did not start there. He started as a shocked young ex-persecutor of the Church, struck blind to the ground by Jesus. He became recognized as an apostle through faithful obedience in the use of his gifting in the calling Jesus had on his life.

Note also that the focus of their titled roles is equipping to do, not simply doing, which would save a lot of burnout! They are to multiply their skills and maturity into the Body, not simply to add their skills to it. Titles are important because they provide easy identification of those who are trusted to help and serve others. But the equippers are no more important or special to God than other titled people—think the janitor or childcare worker. The Church is mistaken when it ascribes titles (or they are self-assumed) to create a sense of importance or rank. It was a key point of anger for

---

*Some think there are only four as the last two grammatically could be thought of as one. In any case, the Church, organizations, and people need all five roles. Let's go with five.

Jesus, who said, "It is not this way among you, but whoever wants to become prominent among you shall be your servant" (Matthew 20:26). Better to downplay the title and focus on serving. These five will be described in more detail in the next chapter.

So what holds all this together? Ah!

Key 5: Ligament Relationships

I remember many years ago when the commute to a downtown church became too long for our young children, and four or five couples decided informally to simply meet in one of our homes. You probably know the story—five families, about fifteen children, and some singles who babysat or lived with some of us. There was no plan to start a "church" church—the plan was just to simply meet together. So many meals together and wonderfully fun stories.

One time, about twenty of us went to Florida together, and we had an amazing game of capture the flag among the dunes under a full moon with pregnant and nursing moms providing the final flag protection circle. We all mist up in smiling remembrance. Then the explosion of growth happened. People began to just show up and invite their friends. The families worked to connect with them and they to each other. The fast-growing congregation ended up buying the school it had borrowed for so long (not wanting to actually be a "church" you understand). Why? One simple word: connection.

That word (and our last key) is Paul's answer to how to grow and maintain a strong Church—better stated, a strong Body of Christ. In verses 15 and 16, Paul, still using the body analogy, talks about each individual in the Body being joined and held together by "speaking the truth in love through 'ligament' relationships." This is the definition of connection, the longing of everyone: speaking loving truth through flexible but unbreakable relationships. A ligament connection.

I once asked a senior pastor friend of a large church how many he "ran on Sunday" (I knew the lingo!).

"Oh," he said, "about 2,500 or so." He looked at me carefully, and knew that I knew that he knew.

So I asked, "How big is the body that meets at your church?"

He smiled wistfully. "That's the question, isn't it? I'm not sure, but probably no more than five hundred. I aim to change that."

"Church" is not the same as "body," though it should be.

In their book *Move,* Greg Hawkins and Cally Parkinson talk about church growth data collected from a quarter of a million individuals in well over one thousand churches.[2] Its findings are somewhat disheartening and related strongly to this key. An important and common issue from that survey is that great speakers and amazing, smoky, rockstar worship can draw a crowd. But often, while there is a sense of enjoying the event and learning good things, there is a feeling of being face-forward disconnected. Those whose experience is only these settings have few, if any, true ligament relationships. Eventually, they simply walk away—or their children do.

Those who have experienced these strong ligament connections with dear friends say the connections are their lifeline. They cherish them. It is wonderful to realize that these connections are exactly what Christ intends.

Only this morning I heard a woman's testimony about how individuals had reached out to her and her spouse. They took them to lunch, connected them with others, and invited them to house gatherings. They lent them a lawn mower and helped them fix their fence. She stated that she and her husband decided to join the church before they had even attended a Sunday service. Connection, mutual connection, created a warm, safe, and loving place for them. They were all in.

When someone encounters a healthy expression of Christ's Body like this, the results seem to have a sense of divine preordination and coordination. They "just happen" to meet the people with whom they need to connect, who just happen to know others whose gifting/ministry is just what they need. And when that person experiences ministry—that connection or love—they feel as if they've encountered Jesus. Why? Because they actually have encountered Jesus, the part of Him that was measured out into a *charisma* gifted person, reinforced by the love and power of the Father bringing holy energy to it all.

We could try to explain these connections as mutual interests, similar life stage or circumstance, living in the same neighborhood, etc., and all those things might be true. But it is Christ who makes all these connections and the fruit of them possible. When we, as a church culture, are observant and understand this truth-in-love dynamic, we far more easily and supernaturally connect with others where there seems to be something special, and even preordained, about a relationship or opportunity to help.

With that God-given concept as a model, the Body of Christ can grow unbounded. It would feel personal and life-giving even if it grew to a million members. As a week-old believer, I had a very moving dream about this. I didn't even know spiritual dreams were a thing. I saw the earth suspended and rotating in space. Small glimmering white lines were growing here and there and meshing across the globe's surface—in all directions more and more. Then, when the whole earth was covered with this white glowing network, a finger reached out from heaven, hooked under a single strand of the mesh, and whooshed it off into heaven. I woke with a start and a yelp—my heart was pounding. The Lord spoke to me to join in the weaving. To this day, that is my vision for the Body of Christ—that vibrant, living mesh.

The five keys described in this chapter by Paul are nonoptional for individuals and the Body corporate. I'm convinced that if local churches and the individuals within them better grasped these keys and began to focus on Jesus' *diakonia* leading in how to live this connected way, then by its very nature, the Body would be strong, growing, and joyful. People would say, as Peter said to Jesus, "Lord, to whom shall we go? You have words of eternal life" (John 6:68).

In the next chapter, we'll discuss ways to get this kind of connection started.

Finding My Ministry

Summary of the Ministry Concept

In the last chapter, we saw Paul's *diairesis* analysis of ministries in the Church and their connection with Jesus. In summary, five keys were given to describe Paul's consideration of the Body of Christ:

Key 1 There is unity that is a gift to be maintained and unity that is a gift to be attained over time.

Key 2 Christ, the head/brain of the Church/Body is both in authority over and connected to each person.

Key 3 Christ measures His essence into each person who, when working within the bounds of that measure, contributes to the whole Body measuring up to the fullness of Christ.

Key 4 Christ has assigned five kinds of mature equippers to shepherd this dynamic of unity and function.

Key 5 Speaking truth through flexible and unbreakable ligament relationships causes the Body to be strong and to
grow without limits.

The five keys that were given by Paul in Ephesians 4 were described so that we could understand how a Christian "career" works
and how the Body of Christ is to function for the health and progress
of each member and the whole.

Before we talk about helpful ways to find our "career path" in the
Body, let's take a quick look at the definitions of the key equippers
within a church setting whose job description is to help us. Read
these with an eye toward identifying those in your life who may
play those roles—identified and titled or not.

The Equippers

In Ephesians 4, Paul lists five types of equippers (sometimes called
the offices) within the Church: apostle, prophet, evangelist, pastor,
and teacher (note that some scholars combine pastor and teacher
into one equipper title; while this may or may not be true, it is true
that pastoral care and teaching are different roles requiring different skills—best discussed separately). When we think of the kinds
of equipping that a church and each individual within it needs, we
see again the genius of Paul's *diairesis* approach and God's design.
I have provided a quick figure to illustrate the five roles.

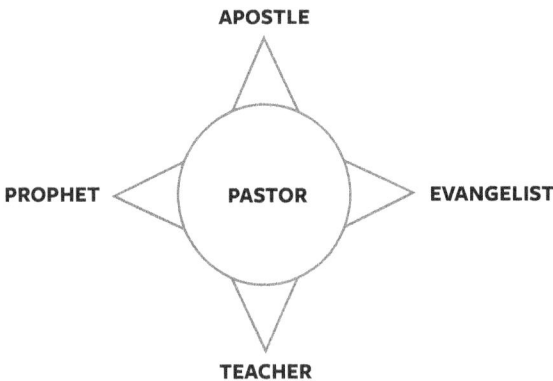

In summary:

- The apostle tends to see far, wide, and up, looking for direction and connection within the larger Church to carry out God's plans.
- The prophet tends, as in the *charisma* gifting, to see where the Church is and what baggage or misdirection it is carrying. In a sense, the prophet looks backward to present.
- The evangelist looks outward, past the boundaries of the Body and into the world that needs Christ and His love.
- The teacher looks at where the Church is in well-rounded maturity and how it can best be grounded in the truth for its calling.
- The pastor looks to the spiritual and emotional health of his or her church members and their ligament relationships, seeking to bring joy and fruitfulness.

Two of the five, prophet and teacher, are also listed among the functional gifts in Romans 12. This can cause some confusion. We would do well to simply think of these two in terms of gifting (*charisma*) and ministry job (*diakonia*) that happen to share the same name, because they represent people who have that gifting and are performing that role.

I often get asked questions like, "Didn't all the apostles and the prophets pass away?" The answer to the question is, "Yes, John was probably the last of the 'Big A' apostles." Paul told us, perhaps a bit tongue-in-cheek, that he, himself, was "not in the least inferior to the most eminent apostles" (2 Corinthians 11:5).

While it is true that the first-century apostles no longer exist, it is also true that the first-century evangelists and prophets no longer exist. First-century Christians no longer exist. Yet the role of each of the five equippers will remain necessary until there are no churches, no need of revival among dying churches, no need to expand to new locations and provide leadership, or no need for prophetic insight, pastoral care, or sound teaching. Every equipping role continues in its various forms until the day you are reading this paragraph because the need for them does not cease.

A common church-culture mistake is that someone takes on the moniker "apostle so-and-so" or "so-and-so prophet of God." This often creates a misunderstanding of the role, and it sometimes promotes a particular man, woman, or ministry. Without judging intention (most are simply a product of their culture), this dynamic causes some people significant distaste for the whole idea of the five-fold ministries. For others, that dynamic causes them to believe they could never be like this great person at the pulpit, so why try? In Matthew 23, Jesus spoke at length about this attitude and behavior among the scribes and Pharisees and concluded by stating, "The greatest of you shall be your servant" (Matthew 23:11). At the end of the Last Supper, He washed the disciples' feet and stated, "So if I, the Lord and the Teacher, washed your feet, you also ought to wash one another's feet" (John 13:14). The loss from this caricature of God's intent is seen in the lack of the equipping that true five-fold ones can create through selfless service moving humbly among a church body.

Here is a more comprehensive description of each of the five.

Apostle

The apostle is the first planter of churches, the visionary entrepreneur, and often a worker of miracles. Jesus named the twelve disciples as apostles before He empowered them with authority, sending them first to the lost sheep of Israel, and then, post resurrection, to all the nations. He sent them in the name and authority He had obtained by His death (see Luke 6:13; Matthew 10:2–6; 28:19). The first apostles (the name literally means "a sent messenger") scattered across the known world creating small gatherings of believers. They equipped those believers in almost every way, watching as God raised up the other four equipping ministries within local congregations.

Within a church setting, apostles focus on direction and connection, equipping the church to expand, interrelate with others, and move on. Even if they are part of church leadership in a single church, they often work informally and relationally among other churches, helping to lead regional expressions and joint efforts. Modern-day Catholic bishops might be an echo of that role. Centralized denominational church leadership can play a similar role.

In *charisma* gifting, most apostles would probably be leaders or exhorters (as Paul probably was), the other two speaking gifts being particularly named as specific ministries.

If a new local church were a company, the apostle would be its founder and first CEO (chief executive officer). At first, they would perform almost every job, but soon the diversity necessitated by growth would appear and they would step back, allowing others to take on equipping and serving responsibilities. If the church were more mature, the apostle would be the one who connects across the city or denomination, providing vision and mature direction for church maturation and the spread of the Gospel.

Prophet

In a five-fold ministry setting, the prophet serves as a highly focused set of insightful eyes and ears. In a place where the prophet is both respected and humbly respectable, there is a wonderful synergy that takes place. The prophet advises leaders and gives insight into direction, correction, and revelation. They may even be a leader or teacher if their arc extends in that direction. They equip all members to better connect with and hear God, to better use the manifestations of the Holy Spirit (see chapter 9), to keep themselves unstained by the world, and to remain free from deception and dark influence. They can typically spot falseness and a counterfeit easily, and they point/call it out for others to deal with. They also have the role of equipping and instructing those who have a similar gift and calling to maturity (sort of like the "company of the prophets" that is mentioned often in 2 Kings).

If the church were a company, the prophet might be the legal advisor.

Evangelist

Remember that these five-fold ministries have as a primary responsibility equipping the Body. Churches thrive when there is a culture of bringing the life-giving truth of Christ to neighbors, co-workers, and cities in ways that build connection. We sometimes can make a mistake when we send the mature evangelist out away from the body, allowing them to be our "missionary" rather than enabling and encouraging the evangelist to create an evangelistic culture within the church—to equip and encourage each church member to be a light in the world.

The evangelist may also help create teams to be sent elsewhere, planting other congregations and bringing the light to other places. A primary value for them is reproducing themselves, their vision, and their fearlessness within the congregation. Thus, their value is not simply being a one-person evangelistic ministry.

If the church were a company, the evangelist might be the sales manager.

Pastor

Pastors (shepherds) have the role of ensuring that church members are mature, healthy, and equipped to bring life and love to others through their ligament relationships. The pastor both cares for individuals and equips the body to care for one another. Typical churches in the last several decades have taken the term "pastor" and added to its original intent. They have made that role the sole "up front" leader and teacher around which the life and direction of the church rotates. "Who is your pastor?" That mistake can have harmful consequences throughout the church. It can lead to limitations and reduce the effectiveness of the other five-fold roles in the church. When one person attempts to fulfill the role of five, they might experience pastoral burnout. This expansion of the pastor's role can also create a narrow-at-the-top feeling that sends others who are called to five-fold ministry looking elsewhere or causes them to think they are "not spiritual," resulting in loss to the Body.

A pastor who understands this concept makes room for all five of the equipping ministries and equips a hundred others to be pastoral. When that happens, multiplication begins. Many body members become equipped to shepherd their families, themselves, their friends, and each other. That is much of the point of speaking the truth in love through ligament relationships. Then day-to-day pastoring primarily takes place one-on-one in families, among friends, and in small-group settings. When that happens, the actual five-fold pastors can focus on making sure the ship is healthy.

If the church were a company, the pastor might be the vice president of personnel.

Teacher

The teacher is the other named *diakonia* that is also a named *charisma*. The five-fold teacher teaches others, but they also teach others to teach. They create an environment in which many are studying the Word and listening to God for themselves and others. The result is that fresh revelation and love for the Word begins to flow through the Body's ligament relationships.

As in each of the five-fold ministries, we can make mistakes in focus and misleading expectations. Teaching is particularly vulnerable to this. When someone is fully taught, they become like their teacher (see Luke 6:40). When a congregation has but one teacher week in and out, they become like them. No teacher provides a comprehensive and balanced diet of the truth; all have blind spots and imbalance. The congregation, as well as each individual, would do well to have many teachers from whom they get the truth, the whole truth, and nothing but the truth.

When we do this teaching multiplication process, many individuals become motivated to study and grow, and more are motivated to sit and listen. Pressure is taken off the teacher to be everyone's source of truth and revelation. He or she does not have to be the one everyone wants to have lunch with. That responsibility shifts to the Holy Spirit in subtle but clear ways. Teachers, like prophets, perform their own *charisma* role wherever they go. They instruct in every setting, large or small. They, too, cannot help it.

If the church were a company, the teacher would be the vice president of training.

With this five-fold structure set up, let's now turn to practical aspects of discovering your *diakonia*.

Finding Your Diakonia (Ministry)

I probably should have entitled this section something different. We may think this subject is a lot like finding a career or a college major. We take aptitude tests, personality tests, IQ and EQ tests, we talk to counselors, and who knows what else. And then we try to make choices among lists of careers. We may be fearful of making the wrong choice. We roll the dice. What if "finding my *diakonia*" is vastly different from that—maybe not even a "thing"? What if?

Think of it this way. If I were invited into the inner circle of a great political or corporate leader and was in daily contact with him or her, there are two things I would want to be very certain of. What is important to him or her, and secondly, what is my assignment. Well, you and I *are* in that position. An all-powerful, all-knowing, and all-loving God has invited us into His family. And He is committed to growing us into someone with whom the Trinity would be pleased to spend eternity. Oh, and to go on crazy, intergalactic missions in the distant future in our new bodies (okay, that last part is speculative). And all of this is done without God dictating our lives to us or violating our free will.

As a young man of 25, discovering my assignment, my *diakonia* career, seemed important, and I spent a good bit of time pursuing it. Then I had sort of a "Duh, Andy" moment. I was reading in Luke about the Transfiguration, where he tells us that the Father's voice came from a cloud and said to Peter, James, and John, who were thinking of building a monument to the occasion, "This is My Son, My Chosen One; listen to Him!" (Luke 9:35). I stopped and had the sudden thought that if I really wanted to know about Jesus and His calling, I should, well, listen to Him.

So I began a habit of having "red letter" days when I read and thought only about what Jesus said—you know, the red letters. That changed almost everything for me regarding finding my Christian career. As I read the words of Jesus, it become very clear that "What should I do?" was of far less importance than "Who should I be?" I realized that if I focused on being the kind of person He *could* use,

I would become the kind of person He *would* use. And I understood that that first part was my responsibility, while the second was mostly His.

Let's talk about that.

Connecting with Jesus and His Word

Remember that Jesus is the head of the Body—both its leader and its brain. From that perspective, the parables of Jesus begin to take on life-changing importance. Hidden in them are the secrets to promotion in His Kingdom—your promotion.

Therefore, the most important first step you and I can take in finding our *diakonia* is to look at what Jesus said, to connect with Him as we do so, and to let those experiences change how we think and go about things—who we are becoming. How do we do that? It's pretty simple. Here are some thoughts that have helped me and others. We'll revisit these when we learn to connect with the Father in the next two chapters.

Ask Jesus if you can be near Him. Think of Jesus in Bible stories and put yourself right there sitting as a disciple of His and watching Him teach, listening. Then, when you read those red letters, let your mind, both the right and left side, visualize and think about them. As you slowly read a Scripture passage, let the verses play across your mind's eye. See them on that inner screen where your imagination plays and where impressions from your spirit and God are displayed. Picture them and seek to hear Jesus in them. Connect and rest.

Let's give it a try. Don't feel the need to say, "God told me that . . ." and don't be afraid. Hold the impressions with an open hand within your heart. Let Him bring them to life in your life.

Let's start with the well-known parable of the sower and the seed. After you've spent a bit of time on your own with the parable, read what I've written below. It is a summary of some observations that have helped me greatly in coming into the *diakonia* plan of Jesus for my life.

The Sower and the Seed (Matthew 13:1–23; Mark 4:1–20; Luke 8:4–15)

◈ Observations

This well-known, organic Kingdom parable is in all three of the parable-containing gospels, and it is one of the few explained by Christ. A man scatters seed wanting it to grow into a harvest. Jesus states that there are three chief causes for lack of spiritual growth to maturity—the three poor soils. Hold up the mirror of the Word to yourself and ask Jesus what you need to know about the soils and your heart.

The roadside where the seed is sown is not conducive to growth, and the devil makes sure it does not produce anything. What life environment or situations do you live within that tend to negate God's maturing work? What are those things that would be counterproductive to spiritual health?

The rocky place is only slightly better. But this person has never made the life-changing decision and acted on it. They don't have life habits of ensuring the truth finds its way deeply and securely. Affliction or persecution will kill the seed in this life. It is targeted to do so. Is your life lived in such a way that a purposeful and consistent place is made for truth and for Jesus' nearness? Have you cleared the rocks from your garden? Look at your bank account and calendar. What do they show? Get still and ask Jesus to search your life and help you get the rocks out. He is very gentle, howbeit thorough!

The thorny place represents the life of distractions, of competing interests, and of a divided heart. The soil is okay, but no effort is made to clear unintended growth. It is too thorny, too hard to clear. Are you allowing anxiety on the one hand and desire for worldly things (or smartphone hypnosis) on the other to choke out the good growth? Jesus says we cannot serve two masters. We should instead have a simple, single-focused eye that results in a light-filled life (see Matthew 6:19–24). Ask Him what you love as much, or more, than Him and His ways within you. Then be still.

Listen over the course of a few weeks. He has a way of suddenly showing you the result or impact of what you just decided, did, or said—always with a warm smile and an invitation to give it to Him.

Always the exchange—death for life. Try a fast from media and see how that goes.

If you especially identified with any of these three counterproductive situations or lifestyles, take a hard look at them. Do so with Jesus. Ask Him to show you what is limiting your intimacy and growth and what His plan is to get rid of it.

The Talents and the Minas *(Matthew 25:14–30; Luke 19:11–27)*

Observations

These two parables are also well-known. They provide additional commentary on finding our *diakonia* calling. There are subtle differences that round out the truth. In the parable of the talents,* each servant was given a *different* amount of money based on his "ability" (which is consistent with his given *charisma* gift and other strengths, including intellect, personality, etc.). They *each* doubled the investment, and each received the *same* reward—being put in charge of many things. The exact amount they made was never compared to that of another servant—only how effective they were with what they were given. That is a game changer for people who think they can never be like another achiever. They are never *expected* to be—at least not by God.

In the mina† parable, each was given the exact *same* amount and received *different* rewards (authority over multiple cities) based on the return on investment obtained by the nobleman. This is a recognition and rewarding of differing efforts and diligence, character traits that are within our purview to change—not gifts and talents.

In each case, *only* the servant who fearfully hid the master's money was punished. In the discussion about *charisma* gifts, Paul discussed the problem of pride and the need to show greater honor to those who lack giftings that attract honor. The opposite direction from pride is the problem with fear or slackness that is discussed in these parables. Only the servant who fearfully hid his gift and didn't make the effort to know the master's love and grace was punished.

---

*A talent was equivalent to the wages of about fifteen years for a laborer.
†A mina was equivalent to the wages of about one hundred days for a laborer.

❋ Gifting and ministry

Everyone is given "talents and minas" to do the things God has called them to do—everyone. We are not given the talents or minas to do things we are not called to do. So it is important to both connect with Jesus around your particular gifting and step out with the fear of the Lord that includes a fearlessness toward the calling and journey.

It is important that you have a pretty good idea about your own *charisma* gift arc. Not perfect. Just a sense of it. As you gain understanding and experience in observing God and your gifting at work in the small and hidden things discussed above, your path forward will begin to seem more clearly marked, and individual yes choices become easier to make.

The next opportunity you encounter seems related to the past things, a bit like a dot-to-dot drawing. Be alert to what sorts of things seem easier and God-empowered that bear fruit and also that may be darkly opposed.

Be careful not to confuse man's requests or opportunities with God's leading. Say a tentative yes to things that feel right on the inside, but be careful of longer-term commitments, unless they seem to clearly be a God-ordained call. Don't worry. God will not waste your time or your gifting. Jesus also faced requests He knew were not for Him (see Matthew 15:24; John 12:20–23).

❋ Mistakes

When you have made an all-in decision and have begun to see through the lens of your gifting, you will have some missteps. The rest of the servants in these parables probably made mistakes in certain ways, but their mistakes were never mentioned. Our Father knows that we will stumble and miss the mark at times (see James 3:2). We are imperfect. That is no problem. It is expected. Just as a baby starts trying to walk and every family member cheers even the falls, God cheers us on even as we make mistakes. Know that there is a "knucklehead" factor built into this dynamic. There is lots of provision for making mistakes. Mistakes are not a problem with God. He just says, "Your life. Take two." You get another take.

The Seed (Mark 4:26–29)

- **Observations**

This parable is not as well-known, being contained only in Mark's gospel. But it carries a powerful message about how God's Kingdom and growing in a mature use of gifting and calling work.

> And He was saying, "The kingdom of God is like a man who casts seed upon the soil; and he goes to bed at night and gets up daily, and the seed sprouts and grows—how, he himself does not know. The soil produces crops by itself; first the stalk, then the head, then the mature grain in the head. Now when the crop permits, he immediately puts in the sickle, because the harvest has come."

- **Things take time in an organic way**

Notice a couple of things. There is an organic nature to the Kingdom of heaven where things grow and come to maturity in "the fullness of time." God's way is not that of the world's siren song that sounds like more, better, different, and now. This happens not because God is slow but because we are. Understand that things can take time, and that timing decision is up to God. We sometimes know why, and we sometimes do not.

- **Faithful consistency**

The man in the parable is faithful in his part. There is a dailyness and consistency to his faith. The crop produced the harvest—the growth of the seed. He wasn't exactly sure *how* it worked, but he believed *that* it worked.

Hebrews 6:11–12 says it this way:

> We desire that each one of you demonstrate the same diligence so as to realize the full assurance of hope until the end, so that you will not be sluggish, but imitators of those who through faith and endurance inherit the promises.

My daily *diakonia* role is to work faithfully and patiently in a called activity or focus area. The success, the harvest, is not my responsibility. I am accountable only for what I can control: my heart and its outworking in daily obedience. Does that feel hard? Here is an amazing, pressure-eliminating fact. "He who began a good work among [or in] you will complete it by the day of Christ Jesus" (Philippians 1:6).

He began it. He will complete it. In His time and in His way. He is all in. Jesus, as the head of the Body and Lord of the universe, is eternally invested in seeing that each one in the Body is involved in meaningful things with Him—not simply for Him. He sees in the hidden, and He rewards in the light. On Judgment Day, Jesus will ask you only one question: "Did you grow into the person I had planned for you to become?" You are never compared to another. You are only compared to your best self.

If you struggle in this area of diligence, ask the Lord if there is a reason for it. Often that reason is a warped view of God, a lack of trust in His faithfulness to us—the sure knowledge that He is good.

The Shrewd Servant (Luke 16:1–13)

⬦ Observations

A servant of a rich man who is about to be fired begins to forgive his master's debtors. While the parable contains other truths, I think the most important things for our purposes are stated almost as an afterthought in verses 10–13:

> "The one who is faithful in a very little thing is also faithful in much; and the one who is unrighteous in a very little thing is also unrighteous in much. Therefore if you have not been faithful in the use of unrighteous wealth, who will entrust the true wealth to you? And if you have not been faithful in the use of that which is another's, who will give you that which is your own? No servant can serve two masters; for either he will hate the one and love the other, or he will be devoted to one and despise the other. You cannot serve God and wealth."

● Unseen faithfulness

Jesus makes a key observation about the heart and behavior of someone who is faithful, though unseen. He says that the one who "is faithful in a very little thing is also faithful in much." And then He gives three categories where such seemingly unseen faithfulness is closely observed by Him: faithful in little—given much; faithful in the use of money—given true riches; and faithful in the use of that which belongs to another—given your own. Faithful in little things, nonreligious things, and another's things. There is no such thing as obscurity. God is watching even when people are not—maybe especially when people are not.

God knows, though the world does not, that premature responsibility breeds superficiality and eventual failure. He starts our *diakonia* career in small and safe ways so that our unintended mistakes are not embarrassing or destructive to ourselves or others. Baby steps. He doesn't want us to fail from the pulpit in front of a thousand people. He would rather we first learn quietly with a few ligament friends. And He watches as He quietly instructs and encourages faithfulness.

I remember a leading female Christian teacher telling the story of being in a book and magazine store and seeing a preacher she knew browsing the skin magazines. She sidled up to him and simply whispered, "God is watching." You can imagine his response. He needed a do-over on that score.

Be faithful when no one is watching and when such faithfulness seems insignificant. Your reward is sure. If that is hard for you, get still and ask Jesus if there is anything He wants to show you about why that seems hard.

The Beginning of the Sermon on the Mount and the Woes
(Matthew 5:1–11; 23:13–29)

● Observations

The "Blessed" list at the beginning of the Sermon on the Mount is a list of things Jesus said were keys to His Kingdom—eight inner characteristics that lead to righteous behavior. Some think they build on one another. They are stated clearly and briefly. They are easy to meditate on and are easy to interact with God about. You can pray, *"Jesus, will You show me if I fall short here? Can You give me a way to freedom and maturity? I want this in my life."* Then simply listen and watch.

Even more interesting (to a geek) is that there are also eight "woes" that Jesus pronounces against the scribes and Pharisees (see Matthew 23). These two lists of eight, the "blessed are" and "woe be to" seem to match each other—one a characteristic of His godly child, and the other the dark counterfeit.

Look at them and envision what each might look like in a familiar life situation. Let them melt into your heart. Ask Jesus where you currently are on the scale between each one and if there is something you can do about it. I don't want to ruin it for you by going over my own blessed/woe list, though the first time I tried it, it was a bit embarrassing. Perfect!

No hurry. You've got time. Remember His organic Kingdom. He sets the schedule for change, and our role is to say yes.

Summary of Finding Your Diakonia

If I could summarize the central, foundational message of all of these words of Jesus, it would be my favorite life verse, Proverbs 4:23: "Watch over your heart with all diligence, for from it flow the springs of life." Jesus states the same thing in Matthew 15:15–20, and He says that the things that flow out of the unclean and wicked heart defile him or her. You are what your heart is. When Samuel was about to overlook David, God told him not to judge based on appearance. God looks at the heart, not the intellect or beauty (see 1 Samuel 16:7).

My job is to develop faithfulness and character right where I am. God's job is to move me from place to place. My job is to be the kind of person God wants to promote in His Kingdom. God's job is that promotion. Want to find and live in your *diakonia*? Watch over your heart. Become the kind of person God looks for. You, too, might go from shepherd boy to king.

I think Frederick Buechner said it best. "The place God calls you to is the place where your deep gladness and the world's deep hunger meet."[1]

There is really one important step in this chapter. Everything else flows from it. Are you in?

Make a One-Time Life Decision

Remember the "one thing"? It is here, too. The only thing that actually can stand in the way of His *diakonia* ministry plan is His deep respect for our free will. We are family, not robots! So if we agree that we also want to walk in His plan for us, His *diakonia* plan is a done deal! Many people waffle throughout their life regarding this concept, and that waffling creates both an inner tension and an open door for temptation and failure.

There are very few sayings from Jesus that are recounted across all four gospels. Those would seem to be sort of the prime directives. In Matthew 10:39, Mark 8:36, Luke 9:24, and John 12:25, Jesus says, in effect, "What good is it if you gain the whole world but forfeit your own soul? If you seek to save your life you will lose it. But if you give your life for Me and the Gospel, you will find it and keep it for all eternity."

And this is not a church thing. It is a life thing. Make the "all in" decision when you are ready. Then renew it almost daily in prayer and simply in conversation with Jesus. Ask Him real-time questions. Listen. He will find a way to communicate with you that is unique to you. Go for it!

The Diagram Continued

In the diagram below, you can see that Paul's analyses fit a particular *diairesis* pattern that we are in the process of uncovering. We are now ready to add the next Level 3 subcategory—the *diakonia* equipper and everyone else.

Now, on to my favorite topic in this whole book—Papa God!

The Spiritual Gifts Blueprint

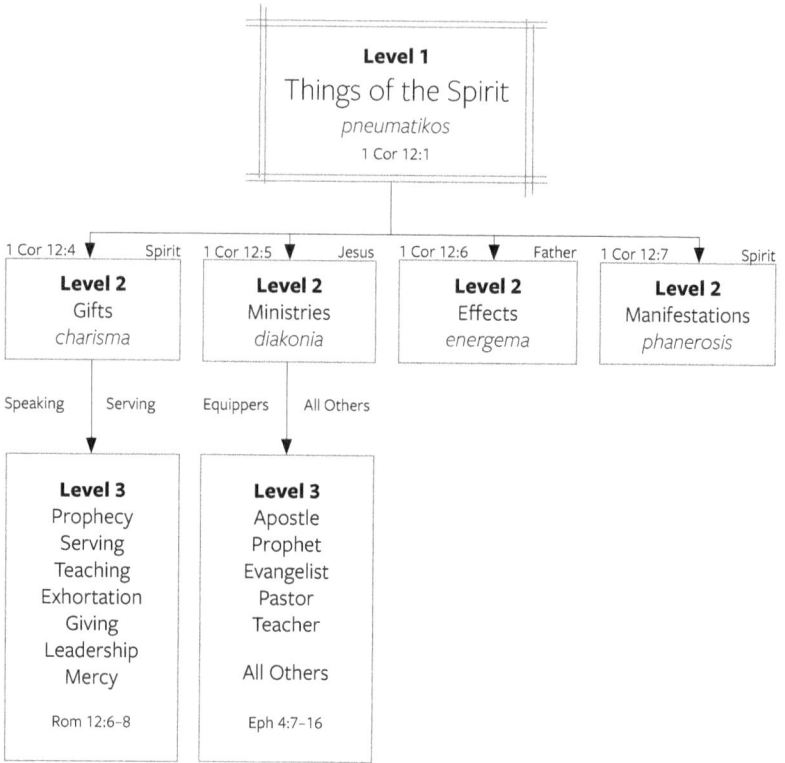

```
┌─────────────────────────────┐
│          Level 1            │
│     Things of the Spirit    │
│        pneumatikos          │
│         1 Cor 12:1          │
└─────────────────────────────┘
```

1 Cor 12:4 ▼ Spirit	1 Cor 12:5 ▼ Jesus	1 Cor 12:6 ▼ Father	1 Cor 12:7 ▼ Spirit
Level 2 Gifts *charisma*	**Level 2** Ministries *diakonia*	**Level 2** Effects *energema*	**Level 2** Manifestations *phanerosis*

Speaking   Serving   Equippers   All Others

Level 3 Prophecy Serving Teaching Exhortation Giving Leadership Mercy Rom 12:6–8	**Level 3** Apostle Prophet Evangelist Pastor Teacher All Others Eph 4:7–16

The Father and Life

Overview

In chapters 3 and 4, we saw that the *charisma* gift arc given to each one of us through the Holy Spirit serves as our basic lens or motivation in any situation. In chapters 5 and 6, we saw our pursuit of our Kingdom career (*diakonia*) worked out by and through Jesus, the head of the Body. In this chapter, we will focus on the third and perhaps least understood component of Paul's *diairesis* analysis of our four-part grace package—the role of the Father in bringing about effects, energized workings, or (to coin a word) "energizings" (*energema*).

The One Thing—Reprise

First things first. Remember the "one thing" from chapter 2? In chapters 3 through 6, we saw that gifting without Holy Spirit connection—or ministry without coworking with Jesus—is often somewhat empty and can only be as powerful as we are. Our results may be good, but they will never be glorious. It is even more important that we start with this idea when considering the Father.

In a send-off gathering for a young missionary couple who were ready to go to Uganda, I said, "You know, God never sent anyone to Africa." While tense looks spread around the room (*What is this old guy doing!?*), the couple smiled because they knew me well enough to know I had more to say. "What I think actually happens is that God says, 'I am going to Africa. Do you want to come along? I would love to have you with Me. I have plans for us.' You are saying yes to that Abba invitation—a bit mysterious and exciting." They nodded, grinned, and clapped because they knew they were called to go *with* God as much as *for* Him. They were getting ready to have an adventure with Dad!

When God calls Moses to Egypt, Moses initially asks the question we all might ask—if we were smart: "Who am I?" (Exodus 3:11). If I were God, I would be tempted to try to convince Moses of his character strengths, his leadership skills, or his past familiarity with the Egyptians. Not God. In reply, what God says is, "I will be with you" (verse 12). While God gives the skeptical Moses more comforting information, a souped-up staff, and Aaron as a companion, God's initial answer seemed to remain His final one: "I will be with you."

With respect to Father God, this idea is expressed in many verses and examples in Scripture. If you look at the calling on the life of almost any God-chosen biblical character, you will see that same amazing expression of God's desire and plan to be with us. In the calling of Abraham (see Genesis 15:1), Jacob (see Genesis 31:3), Moses (see Exodus 3:12), Joshua (see Joshua 1:5), Nehemiah (see Nehemiah 2:8), Isaiah (see Isaiah 41:10), David (see Psalm 23:4), Solomon (see 1 Chronicles 28:20), the disciples (see Mark 16:20), the early Christians (see Acts 11:21), and us forever (see Matthew 28:20; John 17:20), each is told, "My chosen one whom I love. You are called according to My purpose. I'll be with you wherever you go." Paul, recognizing his own experience with this reality, says we are "coworkers" with God the Father, who causes the growth (see 1 Corinthians 3:6–9).

We must grasp this principle. The Father's calling is about connection and partnership—not just sending. Jesus lived in this connected way with the Father, and He repeated this truth with the Father a number of times.

"Truly, truly, I say to you, the Son can do nothing of Himself, unless it is something He sees the Father doing; for whatever the Father does, these things the Son also does in the same way. . . . I do not seek My own will but the will of Him who sent Me. . . . I do nothing on My own, but I say these things as the Father instructed Me. . . . I did not speak on My own, but the Father Himself who sent Me has given Me a commandment as to what to say and what to speak. And I know that His commandment is eternal life; therefore the things I speak, I speak just as the Father has told Me."

John 5:19, 30; 8:28; 12:49–50

And as He was departing, Jesus said an amazing thing about our lives and calling. "Peace be to you; just as the Father has sent Me, I also send you" (John 20:21). And for that "just as" to work, He says He and the Father will come and make their home within us, and the Holy Spirit will fill us and be our companion, helper, and power source (see Luke 24:49; John 14:23, 26; 20:22).

We are all called to live this connected way in every aspect of life. "In Him we live and move and exist" (Acts 17:28). This truth gives us certainty in uncertain times, courage to step out, and comfort when tested. When you read the stories of great men of faith like R. A. Torrey, D. L. Moody, or Charles Finney, each seemed to come to an experience of both the certainty of calling and the uncertainty of what that calling meant. Yet each knew and wrote about the reality of God's presence—and so each stepped out with courage and purpose.[1]

With the "one thing to remember" truth that God will be with us firmly in place, let's move on to Paul's description of how the Father interacts with His children.

Paul's Diairesis Analysis of the Father's Chosen Role

As discussed in chapter 2, Paul states the third aspect of his *diairesis* analyses as, "There are varieties [*diairesis*] of effects [*energema*], but the same God who works all things in all persons" (1 Corinthians 12:6). God the Father provides energy, power, assistance, causation, coincidence, situations, insights, and outcomes for "all things in all persons." All. All. That is very comprehensive. But what does that "all" look like in our lives?

In chapters 3–6 in this book, we have seen that Paul, in his *diairesis* analyses, lists seven primary-color *charisma* gifts (see Romans 12) and five equipping (*diakonia*) ministry roles (see Ephesians 4). And, as we will see in chapters 9 and 10 of this book, Paul's fourth *diairesis* analysis lists nine manifestations (*phanerosis*) of the Holy Spirit (see 1 Corinthians 12). While I don't suppose it's ultimately critical to find, it is interesting to ask, "Does Scripture also present a *diairesis* analysis of the work of the Father (*energema*) as it does for the other three parts of the things of the spirit (*pneumatikos*)?"

I think it does. As is the way of the Father, however, I believe this analysis is there but somewhat hidden. Let's find it.

In his first letter to the Corinthians, Paul declares that love is the most important thing. As he does so, he lists examples of things that God has appointed in the Church that incidentally are not *charisma* gifts, which are focused within individuals, not the Church collectively or when collected together. "And God has appointed in the church, first apostles, second prophets, third teachers, then miracles, then gifts of healings, helps, administrations, and various kinds of tongues" (1 Corinthians 12:28).

Observe that he lists three Ephesians 4 titles (apostle, prophet, and teacher) and three 1 Corinthians 12 manifestations of the Spirit (miracles, gifts of healings, and various kinds of tongues). But he also lists two additional titles: "helps" and "administrations." Unlike the other words on the list, they are not mentioned anywhere else in Scripture.

The word "helps" is from *antilémpsis* in the Greek. From a synopsis of several sources, this word means to "lay hold of for the purpose of helping," and carries with it a sense of strength or authority in so doing. Maybe "authoritative and positive enabling" is a good broad term that matches that fuller meaning. It might look like a father helping or resourcing his child in the processes of getting a summer job, planning and applying for college, or buying a first car.

The word "administrations" is *kybernēseis*, and it carries the idea of one who pilots a ship, who causes things to go a certain way. Maybe "steady and effective steering" is a good phrase. This phrase might be like a father demonstrating and helping his children get started in financial investing, helping to find and negotiate the price for their first car, or coaching his children on how to relate to the opposite sex while remaining godly men or women.

Note that these words imply far more than simple help and guidance. You can't get these things from a book or self-help course. The words imply that there is a sense of quiet but compelling authority, which is with and within us at all times. There is power in the work of the Father for His children that is more than sufficient for the task.

In my long consulting career, I have worked closely with powerful individuals. The most impressive to me were the ones who quietly made the right things happen, negotiated with the right people, changed the minds of the right staff, and convinced the press to print truth. These individuals were quietly and gently unshakable—if you can imagine those words together. They each possessed an undeniable authority that staff and local politicians listened to even as they provided wisdom and direction that tweaked the other participants deep in their consciences. That is our Father.

I have come to the conclusion that the Father's intervention is, to state succinctly, *enabling* and *steering*. He provides what is necessary and guides us in the perfect way at the exact right time to fit each individual learning style, personality, circumstance, and maturity. Yet His work is most often done quietly, and it is hidden behind the scenes. He seems not to force Himself on His children, not to boss them around, not to demand credit, and not to control. We can make mistakes, take a bad direction, and fail—I am proof of that. Maybe you are, too. Honest mistakes, and even some misgivings, are fine with Him. He looks at the heart. It is never too late for the Father to be welcomed into a situation to help bring the desired right conclusion and to work to positively enable and effectively steer it in a way His children could not on their own.

When we gaze across the landscape of Scripture, everything we see the Father doing on behalf of His children can fit into the best sense of these two words. Authoritative and positive enabling (*antilémpsis*) and steady and effective steering (*kybernēseis*).

Hidden God

I have often been asked why I think the Father works in such a hidden way (or "sneaky Dad," as a friend calls Him). I believe one big reason has to do with His loving choice never to ever violate the free will of His children. And if you are the most powerful Being in and outside of creation, that can be a delicate dance.

In earthly relationships, authority (whether it is harsh or benevolent) can work in harmful and controlling ways. That kind of authority is not the Father's way. It seems the Father's primary goal is that we feel at one with Him (see John 17:21)—a comfortable, functional unity. When we recognize this goal, we can see the perfect wisdom of the Father's approach. The feeling of His love and closeness is not overshadowed by His immense power and authority. And when we do experience His work and suddenly realize this perfect combination of love and authority is from Him, we grin and feel deep love and a desire to live all the more with and for Him—like our earthly dad leaving a check and a love note that we find when we unpack our suitcases for our freshman year of college.

Details on the Father's Energema

With the Father's *energema* in Scripture, there is no lengthy *diairesis* discussion as there was with the other three parts of the grace package (*charisma, diakonia,* and *phanerosis*) found in Romans 12, Ephesians 4, and 1 Corinthians 12–14. And equally, it is not possible to list all the key verses that describe, demonstrate, and illustrate all that the Father's *energema* is to His children. Like the Father Himself, it is everywhere and yet nowhere, all at the same time.

So what does *energema* look and feel like? Have you ever noticed someone walking on a moving sidewalk (a people-mover) at an airport? They are not walking faster, but they are moving faster. That is the feeling we begin to get when we purpose to begin walking with the Father. Our *charisma* (see Romans 12) gifting is engaged in our *diakonia* (see Ephesians 4) calling. Manifestations (see 1 Corinthians 12) occur as a matter of course. The *energema* of the Father is around us, in us, and through us. And things happen. Sometimes they are quiet or hidden things, but they can also be head shaking, mouth gaping things. And we smile. Such a fun Father!

He often works through people, most of whom have no idea they are part of His positive enabling and effective steering. I got to play that role when my son and daughter-in-law's home was destroyed by a tornado. They set about to build a unique, A-frame home where the old structure had stood. One day, my son off-handedly mentioned that progress was languishing awaiting a particular permit. I thought, *This is not how this program is supposed to run. And this is my son, whom I love.*

The key staff members in the office that approved permits were long-time personal friends. For years, I had worked as a consultant with them. I called one friend in the office and mentioned the situation. He agreed that there had been an error, and it needed fixing. Twenty minutes later he called me back.

"The permit is signed. Thanks for letting me know. We need to do better." The next day my son stated matter-of-factly that a "miracle" had occurred, and he wondered if I knew anything about it. Well. Maybe. Perfect! *Energema* is sort of like that.

I am far from that perfect dad, and I am far from having control over infinite resources and authority. Yet I did all I could to positively enable and effectively steer the righting of a wrong, and I got to help a deserving and needy person—who happened to be my child. Jesus says if we humans know how to give good gifts to our children, how much more does the Father know and provide for what we need (see Matthew 7:11). How. Much. More. Our Dad is on a first name basis with everyone and everything.

It Is Everywhere

I need to say that this discussion is not just about Christian things. It is about every aspect of life. Jesus lays out this key life principle.

"But seek first His kingdom and His righteousness, and all these things will be provided to you" (Matthew 6:33). And Paul picks up the theme. "And we know that God causes all things to work together for good to those who love God, to those who are called according to His purpose" (Romans 8:28). The effects from the workings of the Father affect your health, thoughts, career, marriage, children, relationships, ministry, and, well, your life.

The book of Acts demonstrates repeatedly this "way" of the Father. In story after story, through hardship and even drudgery, things just seemed to happen. The Father-sent Holy Spirit falls again and again. The cripple is healed. Phillip is transported to speak to the Ethiopian eunuch. The jail doors are opened, and the jailor is saved. "Abundant grace was upon them all" (Acts 4:33). Even when they were scattered because of fear of Paul's persecution, the outcome was a whole region being seeded with life. Paul later walked the same roads watering the seed. We read that a "sense of awe" (Acts 2:43) pervaded the meetings and lives of believers.

And we, too, are participants in this dynamic relationship. When we look back on our lives, we may see many instances of this "causing things to sort of work out." When we are in the midst of a difficult situation, we don't necessarily recognize the Father's positive enabling and effective steering. Then later we say, "That was You, huh?!"

It is amazing to swap life stories with friends. It is almost like a continuation of the book of Acts. Maybe it actually *is* a continuation of the book of Acts! I wanted to tell a bunch of stories from my own life, but that often invites comparison. We tell only our biggest fish stories, anyway. It is better if you and I to begin to understand the Spirit's *charisma* gifting and Jesus' *diakonia* purposes in us and then commit to living in that Romans 8:28 intention to love Him and seek His purpose as our calling. Then we will begin to observe our own stories.

Full Disclosure

Is everything in a Christian's life harps and wine? You know the answer. This *energema* dynamic takes place in the midst of a fallen world whose ruler hates this whole dynamic and works to prevent it, pervert it, and malign it. Just as in the lives of Old Testament characters and of the saints in Acts, in my own story, and in the lives of everyone I know, there are a lot of things causing resistance and trials. We experience many hard, long, or lonely days during which our faithfulness is tested, forgiveness is needed, vision is lost, and the pace is a seemingly slow slog. Those days do not make good stories, but they do make honest ones.

In the midst of teaching about receiving the great hundred-fold blessing of God, Jesus states, "He will receive a hundred times as much now in the present age . . . along with persecutions" (Mark 10:30). Paul tells young believers that it is "through many tribulations that we must enter the kingdom of God" (Acts 14:22). Jesus states, "In the world you have tribulation" (John 16:33). He goes on to say that we can be cheerful because He has overcome the world.

Yet even as we are experiencing the Jesus-described tribulation, we will have a sense of well-being, greater clarity in hearing God, amazement, and inner purposefulness. We will see God move through us stronger and more often. When we trust and cooperate with Father God, He usually takes back far more than Satan steals. Our gifting and ministry will deepen and widen—growing more powerful. As Paul said, and we will begin to say,

> Such is the confidence we have toward God through Christ. Not that we are adequate in ourselves so as to consider anything as having come from ourselves, but our adequacy is from God.
>
> 2 Corinthians 3:4–5

We are the people on that moving sidewalk.

The Diagram Continued

Before we move into the next chapter and look at practical ways to understand how the Father works and how to better connect with Him, let's look at an updated version of the diagram with the concepts we have discussed in the last few chapters. You can now see that Paul's analysis extends the Father's role to the next Level 3 subcategory—the two-part *energema* work of the Father.

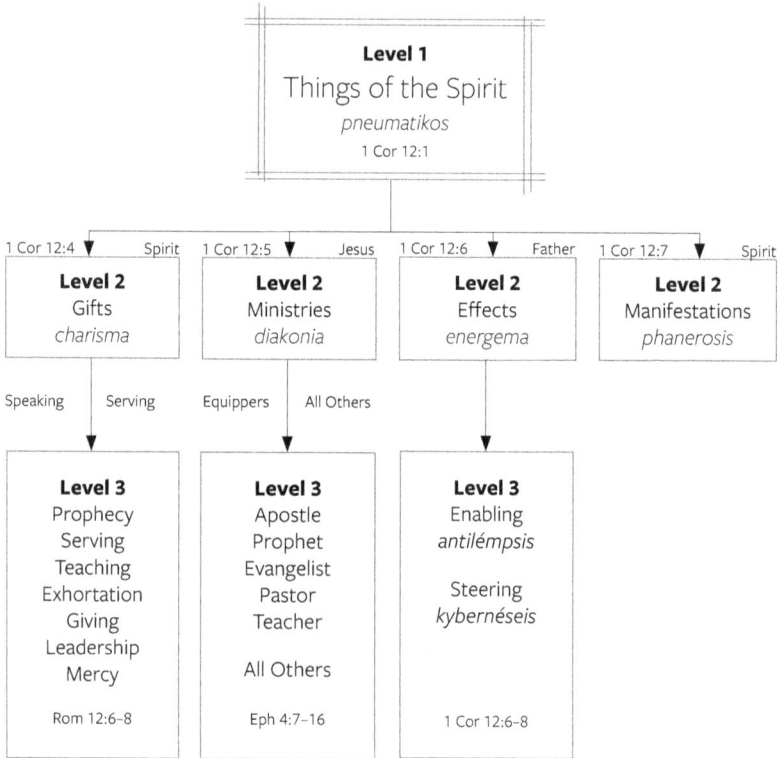

Level 1

Things of the Spirit

pneumatikos

1 Cor 12:1

1 Cor 12:4 ▼ Spirit	1 Cor 12:5 ▼ Jesus	1 Cor 12:6 ▼ Father	1 Cor 12:7 ▼ Spirit
Level 2 Gifts *charisma*	**Level 2** Ministries *diakonia*	**Level 2** Effects *energema*	**Level 2** Manifestations *phanerosis*

Speaking Serving	Equippers All Others		

| **Level 3** Prophecy Serving Teaching Exhortation Giving Leadership Mercy | **Level 3** Apostle Prophet Evangelist Pastor Teacher All Others | **Level 3** Enabling *antilémpsis* Steering *kybernéseis* | |
| Rom 12:6–8 | Eph 4:7–16 | 1 Cor 12:6–8 | |

8

The Father's Smile

Overview

I love the part in *The Lion King* movie when the hyenas are about to devour the two cubs that had strayed into hyena territory. In desperation, the lion cub Simba rears back to roar, and this powerful, hair-raising bellow booms forth—not from Simba, but from Mufasa, the lion king. Mufasa is standing behind Simba, and he makes all the noise and does all the protective work. As it relates to the work of our Father, we are Simba and God is Mufasa. We have Mufasa with us in time of need, which is about all the time! This chapter is about Mufasa.

In the last chapter, we laid out basic information about the third part of Paul's four-part *diairesis* analysis in 1 Corinthians 12—the *energema* or energizings of the Father. In summary, the Father works (most often hidden in the background) on behalf of His children to steer them and with authoritative and positive enabling. In this chapter, we will discuss in practical terms how we can best cooperate and walk with Him.

But first, let's address the elephant in the room. Let's take a look at how we each develop the picture that we have of the Father.

Who Is the Father—to Me?

The idea of living in intimacy with the Father is not a peaceful one for many—at least not at first. This begs the question, Who is the Father to me? Is an encounter with Father God a welcome thing or a scary thing? Let's explore that.

How do we get to know God? How do we hear or encounter Him? Well, apart from Him materializing physically before our eyes, He enters our conscious minds. I believe there are three ways He does that. There are three inner "screens" to which we all, consciously or unconsciously, pay attention. The screen of "senses and drives" is coming from the physical senses and internal drives (hunger, sex, pain from stubbing a toe, etc.) of our bodies. The screen of "memory and analysis" is our mind's ability to recall and analyze. And finally, the deepest is the screen of "imagination and impression," where we can visualize almost anything and where impressions bubble up. These impressions come from our spirit, the place of God's dwelling within us, onto that screen. More on how this works in chapter 10, when we discuss tongues.

To get at the question of who the Father is to me, let's try an exercise that takes advantage of the God-given machinery of that last screen. I have seen this exercise to be effective with hundreds of people. Here is the warmup.* Close your eyes, take your time, and imagine your favorite drink. Just sit with that picture for a moment. You can probably describe it in detail—the frosty glass, the bubbles, the straw, the lemon slices, a mint leaf. You might even begin to smile or see yourself taking a sip. Mmm. Easy to see your drink, huh? We are using one of our three screens (the screen of imagination and impression) to visualize—to imagine.

We can invite God to connect within us using that screen. For example, many of the psalms are David's internal picture on that

---

*Thanks to my friend and ministry partner, Jen Barnett, for this exercise!

screen in his spirit that were given to him by God and written into a song. Psalm 23 is the classic. "The Lord is my shepherd. . . . He leads me beside quiet streams. . . . He sets a table for me in the presence of my enemies" (author's paraphrase).

Christian "mystics" are known for their use of this screen. But using it is not mystical; it is human. And it is God-created to allow Him to visually enter from the realm of the Spirit into our minds and thus into our conscious senses. The process of Him entering our minds and onto this screen is one of the main ways we hear God. It is easy, and even naturally supernatural once we get used to the idea.

Ready? Close your eyes again, still your mind, and imagine listening to me as I say these words: "God the Father." Without slipping into analysis, what feeling, sense, memory, picture, or words come immediately to mind? Pause just a moment. Feel them.

Okay. Let's talk.

Among the hundreds with whom I have prayed and counseled, a common picture I have heard is of someone who is a bit imposing and important, perhaps with white hair and sitting on a throne or in the clouds. Many picture someone who is fairly distant and who is occupied with very important things. The feeling is often like that of seeing the stern face of Abraham Lincoln sculpted in Washington D.C., staring far away and over your head.

In your heart, you know that Lincoln (and the Father) is good. But your picture or feeling makes him seem a bit unapproachable, busy with affairs of state (or of the universe), and your own needs are far less important.

Where were you in that picture? Many say far below, off to the side, or in a crowd—but they are always distant from the Father. The picture feels and seems true. But is it?

Was that far-away impression, that stern image, the one you had? If so, I have good news. Or rather, Jesus has good news.

Restored to the Father

If we look carefully at the life and words of Jesus, we quickly come to realize that a large portion of His ministry, perhaps its entire point, is to show us the Father. He came to show us the real Father, not the caricature we may have had imprinted in our mind (see John 14:8). Not the picture the Jews of His time had. To counter all those impressions, Jesus said things such as, "The Father wants to give you the Kingdom because He loves you. We will come and make Our home in you" (see Luke 12:32; John 16:27; John 14:23). Jesus set about to change everything regarding intimate access to Abba. He did this through both His portrayal of His Father and His own crucifixion. This was done according to the Father's plan to win us from Satan back to Himself. And when we understand that, really understand it, that new reality becomes a most precious possession.

How can that happen?

A life-changing revelation of a good, good Father commonly happens in two main ways.

Approach 1—Jesus: The Picture of the Father

The first is the realization that Jesus is the best picture of God the Father that has ever been seen. If I love Jesus, the step to the Father is a short and easy one. Jesus says, "The one who has seen Me has seen the Father" (John 14:9). Hebrews makes it very clear.

> God, after He spoke long ago to the fathers in the prophets in many portions and in many ways, in these last days has spoken to us in His Son, whom He appointed heir of all things, through whom He also made the world. And He is the radiance of His glory and the exact representation of His nature.
>
> Hebrews 1:1–3

We should question anything we think we know about the Father that cannot be observed in the ways and words of Jesus. Here is what Jen Barnett and I wrote in our book *Freedom Tools*:

> Jesus is God's best, highest, consummate and most accurate expression of the essence of God's character. God's purposes, His gentle yet firm ways among needy men and women, are to be observed in Jesus. His reaction to demonic intrusion is an exact representation

of His Father's. Jesus' response to those caught shamefully in sin is precisely His Father's. The ways of Jesus among brokenhearted men and women unerringly express His Father's heart. His attitude and action toward disease are His Father's. His reaction to hypocritical religiosity, to burdening men with rules and false teaching and to money changers in the Temple exactly mirrors His Father's intense anger.

And Jesus makes one thing *very* clear, *very* simple: "The thief comes only to steal and kill and destroy; I came that they may have life, and have it abundantly" (John 10:10).[1]

I love the idea that Jesus, who is just like the Father, only multiplied three things while on earth: food, wine, and family. I could love a dad like that! Read the red letters in John. If your impression of God the Father looks and feels like stealing, killing, and destroying, it is not the Father. But if it looks like abundant love, open arms, and an invitation to "Come to Me, all who are weary and burdened, and I will give you rest" (Matthew 11:28), then it is probably Abba God—the Father.

Approach 2—Removing the Internal Barrier

The second approach to establishing intimacy with Father God is the idea that since the resurrection and the outpouring of the Holy Spirit, the curtain between mankind and the intimate place of the Holy of Holies has been torn in two (see Matthew 27:51). A way was made to "approach the throne room of grace with confidence, so that we may receive mercy and find grace for help at the time of our need" (Hebrews 4:16). Jesus says, "Fear not, little flock, for it is your Father's good pleasure to give you the kingdom" (Luke 12:32 ESV).

Jesus portrays the Father as the one who is welcoming both the prodigal son and the recalcitrant older brother. He is the one who sent His own Son to make a way for sinners to be intimate with Him. He is the only one who can calm and free our hearts.

Scripture repeats twice that whenever the Holy Spirit influences or fills us, the primary thing He cries out deep in our hearts is "Abba" (see Romans 8:15; Galatians 4:6). Abba is the term a young child calls his or her father. Call Him Dad, Pops, Daddy. These or any nicknames are His favorite names from us, His adopted kids. Our sin and failure are not unimportant. They were so important that Father God took care of them Himself because we could not. While we were far from Him, He came near to us, dealt with our sin and failure, and opened His arms.

We can take His unconditional love very personally! I can ask Jesus to help me see the Father on that inner screen and experience Him. Can I see myself on His lap, head against His chest, perfectly at rest, barging without an appointment into His office, and seeing His welcome smile and open arms (see Hebrews 4:16)? Can I run to, not from, Him when I fail and flounder—seven times seventy times a day? Can I, in the midst of some hard or important point in life, simply close my eyes, nestle, and say, "Abba, I belong to You"?

If our picture from the visioning exercise above of God the Father seemed to portray Him as mysterious, distant, and unapproachable, or if we saw Him as the possible author of untimely death, torment, murder, poverty, hardship, or deception, we need to know why.

The source and origin of those hard and false pictures is typically a combination of the imprint of our childish impressions from our imperfect earthly fathers (we may have received that imprint in the midst of shock from a traumatic father-related experience), our interactions with harsh and distant authority figures, or inaccurate and harsh teaching about God and His children. Normally these impressions are formed in our early years when we had little raw material upon which to base beliefs about reality, and they were then confirmed by the latter experience of a religion in which He is more stained glass than intimate love.

If we ask Jesus why drawing near seems hard, He will show us. We can simply ask, "Jesus, is there anything You want to show me that keeps me from drawing near to the Father?" Often Jesus causes our memory to zero in on one important imprinting event or relationship. He wants to speak truth over the lies that we have believed, and then He asks us to give our lies and wounding burdens to Him so that He can carry them. After all, that is why He died (see Isaiah 53:4).

Uncovering the block between us and the Father may take a purposeful understanding, exposing, and renouncing of any ungodly beliefs that are in the way. We then ask Jesus to show us the truth about the Father. This revelation of the Father is the purpose of inner healing practices and our approach that is used in Freedom Prayer, which has spread to many nations.* Others can be of assistance to us in this process of gaining a truthful image of the Father. The important thing to remember is that this healing can happen, and it is not all that hard. In fact, having an accurate picture of the Father is God's will. And when we know the truth about Abba, things begin to change rapidly.

Get help. It's so very worth it.

Scriptural Examples of This Father God Dynamic

The other half of gaining nearness to the Father is understanding how He works. Among the many verses about the Father's amazing love and faithfulness in steering and enabling, there are a handful that seem to address major considerations in life. They frame truth and give advice on how this dance best happens. We'll use them as illustrations that can serve as way-markers to a far deeper and wider relationship with Father God.

Things Working—God Working Things

Romans 8:28 is typically translated, "And we know that God causes all things to work together for good to those who love God, to those who are called according to His purpose." A second translation approach says, "In all things God works" (NIV). In either case, things get done! We live in a world where God gets the blame for lots of things—lots of "acts of God." But if we have done the inner healing work that is described above to sort out true and false views of the Father, we have fewer problems confusing "abundant life" with "stealing, killing, and destroying."

*See more at www.freedomprayer.org.

This verse has two conditions that we would naturally meet: we love the Father (what's not to love when our picture is clear and biblical) and we are called according to His purpose. This word "purpose" is *prothesis*, and it carries the meaning of setting forth in advance for a specific purpose. It is the Father's preplan for you when He envisioned you before the world was formed (see Ephesians 1:3–6) and you were a gleam in His eye. For my part, if I simply do my best to pay attention to my *charisma* and the *diakonia* of Jesus, stepping into them even with some uncertainty, then this truth about the Father activates in my life. It is the supernatural byproduct of taking the first two steps in the things-of-the-spirit analysis discussed previously. The Father's smile says, "Well done. Let's dance together!"

You don't get a grade. You already passed.

Trials and Temptations

In the world, Christians have trials and tribulation—maybe especially Christians. Who does Satan hate more than sons and daughters of God who are working according to His purposes and guidance, those who are dancing the dance with Him? John says we are tempted and fail in three ways, none of which are from the Father: the lust of the flesh, lust of the eyes, and the boastful pride (see 1 John 2:16). Eve was tempted in these three (see Genesis 3:6) as was Jesus (see Luke 4:1–13), but they battled with opposite outcomes. In Matthew 6:1–18, Jesus gives man three disciplines to build character to counteract these three avenues of sin and failure: fasting, giving, and praying. Fasting counters the lust of the flesh—we are denying the flesh its demand to be fed. And that same ability translates to flesh-denial in other ways. Giving counters the lust of the eyes. I see something I "just have to have" but choose to give away the money I would have spent on that thing. And prayer counters the boastful pride of life when I humble myself, kneeling before God, submitted to Him. Jesus Himself was tempted in every way but remained without sin, and comes to our aid (see Hebrews 4:15).

Far beyond those truths is this: The Father levels the playing field for His children so that in any situation of testing, trials, and temptation we can emerge stronger, smarter, and more joyfully victorious against the wiles of the devil. In the passage below, the Greek word is *peirasmos*, which includes temptation, tests, and trials.

> No temptation, test, or trial has overtaken you except something common to mankind; and God is faithful, so He will not allow you to be tempted, tested or tried beyond what you are able, but with the temptation, test, or trial will provide the way of escape also, so that you will be able to endure it.
>
> 1 Corinthians 10:13

Our Father has limited Satan to those trials and temptations at a low enough level that He knows we have the knowledge and ability to resist or overcome. In a sense, it is the Father, who tempts no one (see James 1:13), who allows Satan only to tempt and test us in a manner in which the positive outcome will strengthen us. There must be the possibility of failure, and that possibility and its consequences are discussed below. But for God's children, Satan and his demons are stuck in a system in which they will most often lose. It is their only option. For us, it is sort of like a workout that will result in strong bodies. This is a soul workout.

And when the pain and darkness of Satan's time-limited authority over this world leads to death, both near-death-experience scientific evidence and history's stories (read Fox's *Book of Martyrs*) seem to prove the compelling veracity of this verse, "Precious in the sight of the LORD is the death of His godly ones" (Psalm 116:15). Think Stephen's martyrdom in Acts 6 and 7. At some point, we will all cross over from earthly to eternal life. Even that is precious to the Father.

Jesus Himself plays a role in this testing and temptation as given by the Father:

> For since He Himself was tempted in that which He has suffered, He is able to come to the aid of those who are tempted. . . . For we do not have a high priest who cannot sympathize with our weaknesses, but One who has been tempted in all things just as we are,

yet without sin. Therefore let's approach the throne of grace with confidence, so that we may receive mercy and find grace for help at the time of our need.

Hebrews 2:18; 4:15–16

How do we apply this truth about the Father's limitation of temptations and tests in daily life? For example, when you and I enter into temptation, our first step should be this thought: "Because of my Father's love, I know I can take this, beat this, and I will be better off for having done so. And my Big Brother is right here to help me."

Once we understand the limits God has placed on Satan, our action step is similar to ambush training. When I was in the military, we were trained that in an ambush you do three things immediately and without thinking: yell AMBUSH, return effective fire, and get out of the kill zone. Three things instinctively. For us, temptation is that ambush. The three clear, reactive, and instinctive things you should do are given in James 4:6–8.

> But He gives a greater grace. Therefore it says, "God is opposed to the proud, but gives grace to the humble." Submit therefore to God. But resist the devil, and he will flee from you. Come close to God and He will come close to you.

This is a quick, ten-second, three-step reaction to testing, trials, and temptation:

1. Submit to God: Place yourself before God with a quick call-out: "Help me please, Father."
2. Resist the devil (not the temptation): "In the name of Jesus, I rebuke you, Satan. You have no authority over me, and I command you to leave me." By the way, it helps, as Jesus demonstrated, to have biblical backing for step two that can be learned and rehearsed ahead of time when you are not in the midst of being tempted.
3. Draw near to God: "Father, thank You that You and I are intimately connected. I choose right now to walk with You

and be near to You—to come boldly to You. Will You show me what that looks like?" Then let the Father speak within you.

When we take these three steps, we become strong, and God's Satan-limiting plan does its work within us. The vulnerable area Satan was targeting becomes stronger and stronger, and we look more and more like our Father.

I have read the end of the story. We win.

And if we fall short? Read on.

Confession and Forgiveness

There are a couple of Bible verses I wish were not true, but they are. James says, "We all stumble in many ways" (James 3:2). John says, "If we say that we have no sin, we are deceiving ourselves and the truth is not in us" (1 John 1:8). But it is a mistake to see ourselves as simply sinners saved by grace. That would be at odds with the Father's view of us.

You might recall the lunchroom movie scene in *Spider-Man* in which Toby Maguire's Spider-Man catches all the flying food in perfect order on a tray. Easy, huh? Well, except for the fact that it took 156 takes to get the scene right.[2]

There are things in my life that require as many takes as that—sometimes more. When Peter asks how many times he must forgive his brother and offers a good round number of seven, Jesus answers, "I do not say to you, up to seven times, but up to seventy times seven" (Matthew 18:22 NKJV). That is 490, if you're wondering.

If God requires that level of mercy and acceptance of others, how much more will He, who intimately knows our weakness, offer it freely to us? The point is that our relationship with God is not about behavior but about heart. And if our heart wants to obey and honor God even when our faltering behavior tells another story, God is good with that. He is all in. We are His family, and there is lots of room for mistakes.

And when we fall short and we sin, we say so.

Confession is, at its essence, an exchange. Jesus bore our sin and its sorrow, and He returns forgiveness, cleansing, and joy. John says: "If we confess our sins, He is faithful and righteous, so that He will forgive us our sins and cleanse us from all unrighteousness" (1 John 1:9). James simply commands, "Confess your sins to one another" (James 5:16). Solomon says, "One who conceals his wrongdoings will not prosper, but one who confesses and abandons them will find compassion" (Proverbs 28:13).

Society's habit is to hide its sins and shortcomings by pretending that they don't exist. God gives us strong reasons not to hide our faults.

> When I kept silent about my sin, my body wasted away through my groaning all day long. . . . I acknowledged my sin to You, and I did not hide my guilt; I said, "I will confess my wrongdoings to the LORD"; and You forgave the guilt of my sin.
>
> Psalm 32:3, 5

Sometimes it is sufficient to simply confess to the Lord and ask Him if it would be okay if you gave your sin to Him. Don't forget to ask Him what He wants to give you in return. But when you least want to expose some "horrible, dark, slimy thing" about yourself, it is important to have that "ligament relationship" (described in Ephesians 4 and chapter 5), in which you can share your worst and hear truth spoken back in gentle love.

Failure and confession are sometimes the fastest way to grow. The way down is the way up. I have a friend with whom I am truthful about my sin, and nothing is hidden or minimized. I lay it out without excuse or self-shaming. My friend pronounces the truth that confession results in cleansing and freedom—not the shame and marginalization I might have imagined. He tells me he is proud of me. He reminds me that I am a beloved child of God who has taken a misstep—not the rightful target of the dark, defining accusation of Satan. And Satan loses again.

Find friends like that, and learn to be one.

Exchanged Anxiety

The Father knows that it is easy for His children to worry and be anxious. Jesus spoke about this topic often and deeply. He enters a discourse on worry and on the role of the Father in caring for His children (see Matthew 6:25–34; Luke 12:22–31), and then He ends with this classic truth about the Father:

> Therefore do not be anxious, saying, "What shall we eat?" Or "What shall we drink?" Or "What shall we wear?" For the Gentiles seek after all these things. For your Heavenly Father knows that you have need of them all. But seek first the kingdom of God and His righteousness, and all these things will be added unto you.
>
> Matthew 6:31–33 BLB

What a wonderful exchange! I get to seek first God's Kingdom and His character, both of which are a huge plus to any human. In exchange, everything the world chases after is given at the right time and in the right way by the Father.

Philippians 4:6–7 shows us how to handle anxiety in the heat of the moment:

> Do not be anxious about anything, but in everything by prayer and pleading with thanksgiving let your requests be made known to God. And the peace of God, which surpasses all comprehension, will guard your hearts and minds in Christ Jesus.

Again, the key is an intimate, real-time connection with the Father. When anxiety arises, we look objectively at it and then turn to the Father for what we need. We connect with Him and ask Him for what we feel we need, allowing His answers and guidance to be wiser than our requests. Then, we look inside for the place of peace.

For many of my friends, or those with whom I've had the privilege of engaging in inner healing, they receive a picture of connection. Examples of this have been walking on the beach, sitting with Him, standing close by the throne, or sitting on His lap. There is often an exchange such as "Cast all your anxiety on Him, because He cares about you" (1 Peter 5:7).

Someone is led to ask, "Father (or Jesus), can I give this burden to You? It is too heavy for me to carry." On the inner screen, the responses have been so amazing, personal, and surprising that those who are witnesses to these answers often marvel, speechless.

Rescuing a drowning man is important. But teaching him to properly swim before he ventures into deep water is better. Paul uses this order of instruction with his words on anxiety and peace. After Paul's "heat-of-the-moment" instructions, he states that we should prepare before we are in the anxiety battle. We should practice this thought discipline:

> Finally, brothers and sisters, whatever is true, whatever is honorable, whatever is right, whatever is pure, whatever is lovely, whatever is commendable, if there is any excellence and if anything worthy of praise, think about these things.
>
> Philippians 4:8

Practice makes perfect.

Work and Reward

The next key truth framing how we connect with the Father has to do with our daily work and career life. Father God is interested and involved in every aspect of our lives. There is no such thing as "religious" and "secular" in His Kingdom. It is all His. The section on anxiety gave an amazing general truth, "Seek first His kingdom and its righteousness and all these things will be added unto you" (Matthew 6:33). The phrase "all these things" includes the Father's watchful blessing over our purposes in life—including how we spend our days and how we make a living.

In the last chapter, I mentioned there were many happenings in my own life that made me cry with joy at the Father's lavish love. When I think back on the big things, the most surprising things, most had to do with what felt like undeserved recognition and advancement in my engineering practice or direction and connection in my ministry. It felt like being spoiled.

When you look at the Old Testament heroes, much of the narrative is about the Father prospering them and evil attacking them. This includes Israel in Egypt, Joseph, David, Daniel, Abraham, Moses, and so on. Again and again, the story was prospering, hardship, attack, hatred, rescue, and growth.

God's part in this narrative is to prosper us. That is His promise. Ours is first to seek His Kingdom and His righteousness as top priority. But then we must not forget that we are to work hard, to work well, and to observe how the Father wants to cause our employer to prosper through us. Christians should be the most cherished employees and business owners on earth.

> Whatever you do, do your work heartily, as for the Lord and not for people, knowing that it is from the Lord that you will receive the reward of the inheritance. It is the Lord Christ whom you serve. For the one who does wrong will receive the consequences of the wrong which he has done, and that without partiality.
>
> Colossians 3:23–25

Lazy, sloppy, shoddy, nondiligent work is an affront to the Lord and our representation of Him to an employer. Paul is clear that there are hard consequences for such behavior, and God shows no family partiality. As His children, we should set an example of excellence and diligence.

The Father's Three-Part Guarantee

There is a last thing I want to share about how we think through life and the Father, and that last thing is His guarantee on eternity. I was listening to a discussion among some college students about destiny. The questions in their minds seemed to revolve around what destiny God might have for them when they got older. I just had to speak up.

"I can tell you exactly what God's destiny is for you." There were shocked looks all around. Was I some kind of fortune teller? Nope. I told them that Father God had already answered that question so that they would not have to worry about it. The answers come directly from Scripture, and they apply to you as well.

- You will be like Him. "For those whom He foreknew, He also predestined to become conformed to the image of His Son, so that He would be the firstborn among many brothers and sisters" (Romans 8:29).
- You will be with Him. "He predestined us to adoption as sons and daughters through Jesus Christ to Himself, according to the good pleasure of His will" (Ephesians 1:5).
- You will share all His stuff. "In Him also we have obtained an inheritance, having been predestined according to the purpose of Him who works all things in accordance with the plan of His will" (Ephesians 1:11).

"Destiny" from God's perspective is rarely about this life—that is way too shortsighted. Father God wants to ensure that we never need to be anxious about our future. It is like a good father who tells his children he has already saved for their college education. Their only job is to do their best in school. Since eternity is secure and our destiny is sure, we can then be free to make this life about discovering daily what amazing and God-ordained thing He wants to partner with us in—the works He has prepared for us. The real question is, What is your purpose here?

Dear ones, we each have a powerful Holy Spirit and a strong gifting, we have Jesus and an exciting ministry calling, and we have a Father who is a sure support along our path from glory to glory. They are committed to connection with us, to walking with us, and to growing us up into Kingdom children. We can choose connection with them. We are in training for eternity, after all. We will be together for a long time!

Derri's Story

In closing this chapter, I wanted to share a story from a dear friend. It speaks for itself about the goodness and amazing choices of the Father. He knows us better than we know ourselves, and He always, always comes to us from our destiny—not from our history. Here's Derri!

It would be hard to imagine a less likely candidate for starting a nonprofit addressing human trafficking in my state than me. I've no training, wealth, influence, connections, notoriety, or glamor. I'm as ordinary as they come. But God cared about the unserved victims and unrecognized issue of human trafficking in the region I live in, and He invited me along to do something about it. It wasn't a last-minute invitation. He planned this for me since before the creation of the earth and made me for the task. In fact, twenty years before the start of this nonprofit, a stranger from New Zealand walked into a crowded Bible study, targeted me, and quietly said, "God will use you to set many women free." I had no idea what that meant, but I knew it was God, and I treasured it in my heart. Though at many times I was overwhelmed by the message, this word reminded me that it was God who called me, equipped me, and went before me.

I have a strong, lifelong desire to right what is wrong and to improve what can be made better. When I was in kindergarten, my nickname was "Bossy Cow," which was the first hint at my gifting. Without my knowing what to call the arc of this gift of leadership with the wing motivation of prophecy (righting what is wrong), God stirred up my indignation about human trafficking and brought me alongside Him to act—starting with nothing and doing everything myself.

I was soon joined by a ragtag group of volunteers and later by professional staff. I was, and still am, in awe of the incredible favor and guidance God gave me every step of the way. At first, everyone with influence who I talked to said, "That doesn't happen here." Today, legislators eagerly sponsor the bills that we propose to fight human trafficking. State agencies turn to us when a victim needs care. And the model of care built by God's grace is recognized and emulated nationwide. Well over a thousand survivors of human trafficking have now received help to rebuild lives. And this week, the state of Tennessee announced it was giving us a whole multimillion-dollar campus perfect for that recovery.

I was given incredible favor and resources to carry out the task. I didn't have training but unknowingly walked in the center of my gifting, felt Jesus stir a ministry call within me, and watched Father do all the heavy lifting. Was that manifestation of the Spirit, that word of knowledge spoken decades ago true?

Maybe so.

With the first three things of the spirit in mind, let's now turn to perhaps the most controversial aspect of this grace package: the manifestations of the Holy Spirit.

The Holy Spirit
and Manifestations

Overview

In the last six chapters, I laid out the first three parts of the Trinity-empowered basic grace package (*pneumatikos*) for each believer: my gifting (*charisma*) and the Holy Spirit, my Kingdom ministry (*diakonia*) and Jesus, and the enabling and steering presence (*energema*) of the Father. In this chapter, I will focus on the last pieces of the four-part grace package, which are the manifestations (*phanerosis*) of the Holy Spirit. Paul is finally getting to the answer to the question the Corinthians probably asked concerning proper and orderly use of manifestations within their gatherings. The details of his answer are found in 1 Corinthians 12–14. He begins that discussion by listing and giving his *diairesis* analysis of the nine manifestations of the Holy Spirit.

> [7]But to each one is given the manifestation [*phanerosis*] of the Spirit for the common good. [8]For to one is given the word of wisdom through

the Spirit, and to another the word of knowledge according to the same Spirit; [9]to another faith by the same Spirit, and to another gifts of healing by the one Spirit, [10]and to another the effecting of miracles, and to another prophecy, and to another the distinguishing of spirits, to another various kinds of tongues, and to another the interpretation of tongues. [11]But one and the same Spirit works all these things, distributing [*diaireó*] to each one individually just as He wills.

1 Corinthians 12:7–11

The word for "manifestations" (*phanerosis*) here means a "clearly visible work." It comes from the word meaning "to shine."[1] The manifestations given by Paul are the word of wisdom, the word of knowledge, faith, gifts of healings, the effecting of miracles, prophecy, the distinguishing of spirits, various kinds of tongues, and the interpretation of tongues.

It should be noted that this list is not singled out and specifically called "gifts" (*charisma*), as is the listing in Romans 12. But when it is referred to alone, it is termed "manifestations" (*phanerosis*). It appears in 1 Corinthians 12 that Paul is distinguishing this list from the other three "things of the spirit" (*pneumatikos*) and that the four lists are not just "gift listings" but are different in kind. They are not comparable, nor are they the same. Referring to these different categories is not like saying we have big and small cans of paint of different colors. It is rather like saying we have paint, painting jobs, painting successes, and different painting tools. This list is the tools.

This understanding doesn't correlate with the general practice in parts of the Church where this nine-item list is called the "gifts of the Spirit," but it seems to correlate far better with the specifics of Scripture.

I wish Paul had been more consistent and limited with his use of the word *charisma* or *gift*. The basic Greek word *charisma* in its five forms is used seventeen times by Paul for the bestowed grace of God. In each instance it is clear what he is referring to, and those references are not equivalent. Thus, the context of what he is saying determines the specifics of definition. The Romans 12 context is clear and definitive. Gifts there tend to be associated with your function. Tongues or a word of wisdom would not fit that idea despite Paul's blanket use of the "gifts" term in 1 Corinthians 12:31. Hold that thought for now and see how this works out.

More on that in Appendix A.

Definition and Descriptions

Note that in 1 Corinthians 12:11, Paul uses the verb form of *diairesis*. Recall from chapter 2 that this word carries with it the meaning of "a distinction arising from a different distribution to different persons," and was used to describe a thought process by which Paul came up with a listing of each of the other three components of things of the spirit. What I think he is saying is that the Holy Spirit distributes manifestations as He sees fit, and that, in Paul's own analysis, there are nine basic categories of these manifestations. Like *charisma* gifts, these are best thought of as points along a continuum, markers for clarity rather than limitations on variability. They are the "primary colors" of manifestations.

Here are brief descriptions and scriptural examples of possible occurrences of each of the nine. Appendix D provides a more detailed description of each one and its use. Chapter 10 discusses tongues and prophecy in applied detail, which mimics Paul's approach with the Corinthians in 1 Corinthians 12–14. This tongues and prophecy discussion will be important as those two often serve as a basis, or proving ground, for future use of the other manifestations. If we get those two right, the others follow along much more comfortably.

Some manifestations (tongues and prophecy) are "at will" and are widely distributed in churches worldwide. A believer can speak in tongues or prophecy at any time. Some (often word of knowledge and wisdom) are partially at will in that an experienced believer can influence them to arise through confident expectation.

Various Kinds of Tongues (Acts 2:4; 10:46; 19:6)

Surprisingly, scientific study shows that the ability to speak in tongues is probably a human capability that God uses to carry the flow of revelation and/or prayer from our spirit, bypassing our cognitive brains, and coming out in "speech." (More on that in the next chapter.) Tongues appears to be both a God-prompted and an "at will" manifestation, and this gift seems to have two matching purposes: to communicate God-prompted truth when interpreted, and to pray or worship privately at will.

The Interpretation of Tongues (Acts 2:8; 10:46)

The supernatural occurrence of the interpretation of tongues is the giving of the "sense" or "meaning" of a spoken tongue—whether yours or another's. The interpretation is distinguished from "translation," which is a word-for-word rendering. Tongues plus interpretation can amount to the next manifestation: prophecy.

Prophecy (Acts 7:2; 11:28; 13:2; 19:6; 21:4, 11)

The supernatural occurrence of prophecy is speaking the thoughts or words of God to others. Prophecy is almost never a word-for-word robotic mimicking and does not need to foretell the future (which might better be termed a "word of knowledge," which is described next). Prophecy is described as speaking God-initiated thoughts to men for edification, exhortation, and consolation—a forthtelling (see 1 Corinthians 14:3).

The Word of Knowledge (Acts 5:3; 8:26; 9:10; 10:5; 16:6–7, 9; 18:9; 20:23; 23:11; 27:10, 23)

The supernatural occurrence of the ability to know, and to speak out, specific information about a person, situation, or thing by revelation of the Holy Spirit apart from, but not necessarily contrary to, our natural senses or normal sources of information.

The Distinguishing of Spirits (Acts 8:21; 13:9; 16:16; 17:16; 19:17; 22:21)

The supernatural occurrence of the ability to perceptively distinguish among or provide a judicial estimation on spiritual sources: human, demonic, angelic, or divine. The distinguishing of spirits often involves an assessment of the mixture, motivation, or intent of the sources.

The Word of Wisdom *(Acts 3:24; 6:10; 9:15; 10:15; 13:46; 14:22; 15:28; 17:22; 21:23; 22:21; 23:6)*

The supernatural occurrence of the ability to know or understand the ways and/or plans of God for a specific situation, and to speak the words out in such a way as to articulate the wisdom of God in the situation.

Gifts of Healings *(Acts 3:6; 5:16; 9:18, 34; 14:10; 19:11; 28:8–9)*

The supernatural occurrence of the ability, through some action, word, or prayer, to bring about or serve as a conduit for healing in a specific situation or situations. History and observation support both different modes of operation for healing and different types of healing—thus the double plural of the title.

The Effecting of Miracles *(Acts 5:12; 6:8; 8:6; 9:40; 14:3; 16:26; 19:11; 20:10; 28:6)*

The supernatural occurrence of the ability to interrupt the natural world order or physical laws by God's power to bring about His intended action or purpose.

Faith *(Acts 4:19, 29; 7:56; 14:9)*

The supernatural occurrence of the ability to believe for a specific thing in a specific situation beyond one's own normal ability or faith because of a revelation or the empowering of God for that situation.

Key Truths

Below are five keys to understanding and properly using manifestations. I wish someone had shared these with me in the 1970s when I, and others, began to experience them. I think we each made nearly every possible mistake by not knowing these keys—some several times! So take time to digest them, envision them, and live by them in this area. It will save you lots of trouble, trust me!

Key 1: Humility and Lack of Show

Recall that 1 Corinthians 12:7 says each one is given manifestations (by the Holy Spirit) for the common good. There are no "haves and have nots." It is important that the manifestations, especially the most powerful ones, are humbly and thoughtfully used by the ones given such responsibilities—and that no one conflate the power tools with maturity, position, revelation, and promotion. Such misuse has caused turmoil in some and stunted the growth of manifestations in others—especially in more conservative expressions of Christianity.

These manifestations are "supernatural" but not "unnatural." That is, they can often seem to flow easily and comfortably up from our spirits into our minds and out into the world through words and actions without great fanfare or the use of King James English. They are to be part and parcel of the life of every Spirit-aware believer. It is better for the recipient of a manifestation to become individually aware that God has done something than it is to have that thing announced.

Key 2: Owners and Users of Manifestations

Unlike the other three *pneumatikos* categories, most manifestations are a human action prompted in real-time at the initiation of the Holy Spirit within our spirits. The manifestation is the "power tool," and the person is the one needing or employing that particular tool at that time. The use of the manifestation is generally under the control of the user, but the owner is the Holy Spirit, not the person. In a sense, a manifestation is on loan from the Holy Spirit. That is why, in each definition above, I have used the introductory phrase "the supernatural occurrence of the ability to." While some manifestations are "at will," it is sound wisdom to consider manifestations as a partnership arrangement with the Holy Spirit rather than an ownership-by-me arrangement.

Key 3: Unpredictability of Manifestations

Manifestations "happen" at a point in time. Sometimes even the one through whom the manifestation flows is surprised. They can be unpredictable. Scholar N. T. Wright calls the how, when, and why of the manifestations, especially the most powerful ones, a mystery, and one that will probably remain so.[2]

Let's use healing as an example. Peter's shadow did not always heal everyone—but it did once. Healing did not happen for everyone who desired to be made well by Paul, but it often did (see 2 Timothy 4:20). Noted healer Francis MacNutt and I had a discussion about this issue many years ago that helped my understanding. In a 1991 article in *Healing Line*, he lays out this mature and kind analysis of this issue. If you would like a balanced representation, I recommend you check out the article.[3]

In looking at "why" a manifestation did or didn't happen, there is no clear rule or set of practices that can make something happen like clockwork. It is not like a shaman casting a spell or curse. Any person can potentially be used in any manifestation. As proven by the Corinthians, manifestations do not seem to depend on maturity. Sometimes there is something that the charismatic world calls an "anointing" for a certain manifestation, and that anointing can come and go. It does not depend on maturity as much as earnest desire and God's sovereign choice. As noted healing leader, Bill Johnson, has joked in my hearing at Bethel Church in Redding California, "Even jerks can be anointed."

In my own life, there was a six-month period during which everyone I prayed for shook and felt tingles—many fell to the floor. I could guess at reasons for that, but I had no air-tight reason why. There have been many instances when someone young and inexperienced has been given an anointing for some manifestation that seems unusual. For example, in 1977 in Virginia, in a Catholic charismatic setting of which I was a part, a young girl began to pray for those who wanted to quit smoking. It began when she told the priest who was holding her that she hated his breath. He said, "Well then, young lady, pray I can stop." She did and he did. As I watched that night, everyone she prayed for developed a distaste for cigarettes and was easily able to stop. This continued over a period of a month or so. They all said that they had no more desire. Maybe childlike faith is what it takes!

Key 4: A Faith Atmosphere

An "atmosphere" of faith can be seen as a key, though that argument can quickly move into shaming and accusations, which would be wrong. With that in mind, here is a scary thought: Even Jesus, the King of kings and Lord of lords, was without power to heal in His hometown. He tried and failed. He marveled at the level of their caustic unbelief toward Him—their homegrown carpenter's son (see Mark 6:1–5). Yet He, equally, but in an opposite sense, marveled at the unexpected great faith of the centurion. This man had a revelatory explanation about how he came to believe Jesus could and would heal (see Matthew 8:5–13). A friend who has a long history of healing said, "Any evangelist can heal in Africa. Just try it in America." A team from our Freedom Prayer ministry was recently in India teaching and demonstrating the ministry techniques.[4] The team leader told me that one afternoon as they were ministering, the miracles began. They saw a number of clear and instantaneous healings. Even though the team was ministering in a still and hot room, they watched as a woman, who had been freed from shame, experienced a sudden wind that blew the veil away from her face. The ministry team returned as different people. I hope they never change back!

It is a mistake to assume that because we may not have experienced seeing the miraculous it is not for today and not for us. As has been demonstrated many times, manifestations can happen anywhere. Even when a simple faith is expressed in halting words.

Key 5: Filling with the Holy Spirit and Manifestations

It would be a needless distraction to enter into a long discussion about the topic of the "baptism in the Holy Spirit" or "filling with the Spirit" and the various belief systems at play. For many believers, however, finding a comfortable and biblical understanding about that topic is important to enter the reality of Holy Spirit manifestations. Let me simply share the stance I arrived at many years ago that has served me well across the decades and the spectrum of churches I discussed in chapter 1.

Jesus provides a definitive statement about the giving and reception of the Holy Spirit.

> "The one who believes in Me, as the Scripture said, 'From his innermost being will flow rivers of living water.'" But this He said in reference to the Spirit, whom those who believed in Him were to receive; for the Spirit was not yet given, because Jesus was not yet glorified.
>
> John 7:38–39

At Pentecost, Peter states categorically that the Holy Spirit has been poured out because Jesus has been exalted. He states that the Holy Spirit, however experienced, is for all believers in all ages.

> "Therefore, since He has been exalted at the right hand of God, and has received the promise of the Holy Spirit from the Father, He has poured out this which you both see and hear. . . . Repent, and each of you be baptized in the name of Jesus Christ for the forgiveness of your sins; and you will receive the gift of the Holy Spirit. For the promise is for you and your children and for all who are far away, as many as the Lord our God will call to Himself."
>
> Acts 2:33, 38–39

The Holy Spirit was poured out and made available to all believers because Jesus was glorified. No other reason. And the Holy Spirit is given to us when we are born again—or we could not be born again (also known as being born of the Spirit). No question. Most conservatives would say that it is finished. We don't get just part of the Holy Spirit—or do we?

Yet many believers, including the apostles,* also point to a time and event that is post baptism when they begin to experience

---

*Jesus breathed the Holy Spirit into them in John 20:21–22, yet in Luke 24:49 He told them to remain in Jerusalem until the Spirit filled them with power from on high. There are other biblical explanations for this two-part filling as a special case.

manifestations, often accompanied by a sense of a fresh filling of the Spirit. Their experiences, however, are widely diverse. Pentecostals and charismatics may call that experience the "baptism in the Holy Spirit" or a "second work of grace" and conclude it is a necessary one for Christian maturity and power.

Ephesians 5:18 is the classic verse comparing the euphoria of too much wine and the filling with (or by) the Holy Spirit. "And do not get drunk with wine, in which there is debauchery, but be filled with the Spirit." Some would argue, perhaps thinking of Acts 13:52, which describes the disciples being continually filled with the Holy Spirit, that the best translation is "but be being filled with the Spirit."

Note the posture of constant filling, constant flow—not a one and done. It seems even Peter and Paul were filled several times in the book of Acts (see Acts 2:4; 4:8, 31; 13:9, 52).

D. L. Moody was once asked why he urged Christians to be filled constantly with the Holy Spirit. "Well," he said, "I need a continual infilling because I leak."[5] I have come to observe and believe that a posture of continual desire for and openness to the flow and filling of the Holy Spirit within and through us is the best way to enter into the manifestations in our lives. I believe in a "second blessing," and a third and fourth and . . . I've lost count. "More, Lord" is a great stance.

Manifestations of the Spirit: Organization

It is always a bit dangerous to organize things—and the Bible does not specifically organize the manifestations. But with that caveat in mind, let's look at a systematic way of grouping the manifestations that has proven to be helpful in bringing clarity and understanding. The manifestations of the Spirit can be thought of as appearing in three related and ordered groups:

1. tongues, interpretation of tongues, and prophecy
2. the word of knowledge, distinguishing of spirits, and the word of wisdom
3. gifts of healings, effecting of miracles, and faith

KNOWING

Word of Knowledge,
Distinguishing of Spirits,
Word of Wisdom

DOING

Gifts of Healings,
Miracles, Faith

SPEAKING

Tongues, Interpretation
of Tongues, Prophecy

We might think of these three groups as featuring speaking, knowing, or doing, as indicated in the figure.

Group 1—Speaking: Spirit Connection

The initial three (tongues, interpretation of tongues, and prophecy), as observed in the book of Acts and in experience, often seem to serve as a foundation or as an introduction to the others. But there are no firm rules. As demonstrated above, even young children can exhibit the more powerful manifestations without starting with these. These three each involve inspired speech. They are sort of "Manifestations of the Holy Spirit 101" and have to do with simple Spirit connection. They were the signs of Spirit filling in the book of Acts.*

Because of the foundational importance of tongues and prophecy, I will summarize here and provide a more detailed description in the next chapter. Speaking in tongues does not require anything to actually happen in the realm of conscious understanding. Tongues being used personally is quite common. According to 1 Corinthians 14, we speak mysteries, give thanks well enough, etc., but, when we speak in tongues, we don't really know what is being said. Paul states that his spirit speaks but his mind is "unfruitful"

---

*See the accounts in Acts 2; 8–10; 19.

(1 Corinthians 14:14 NIV). Speaking in tongues is, in many ways, a great introduction to the spirit realm (versus the realm of the soul) because our mind is out of the picture. It is no longer in control.

In interpretation of tongues, the responsibility for what is said is "shared." One speaks in a tongue and another, or the same individual, gives the sense of what is said. The translation is not a word-for-word interpretation. In this way it is easier than prophecy and more demanding of individual accountability than tongues alone. Some have said that they often only get the beginning of what is to be said, like a thread. When they begin to speak, the rest is tugged along.

Prophecy occurs when people speak and share what they feel the Holy Spirit has prompted them to say. While you must take responsibility for what you hear and say, the prophecy (not you) is to be judged by others (see 1 Corinthians 14:29). In that sense, prophecy may require more faith and the ability to hear clearly in the spirit than the first two manifestations. But, as Paul states the balance, "we know in part and prophesy in part" (1 Corinthians 13:9) and "do not utterly reject prophecies" (1 Thessalonians 5:20).

With prophecy, the speaker is giving a forthtelling word of edification, consolation, or exhortation that carries a sense of God's influence, not a foretelling word about the future (see 1 Corinthians 14:3). Yet prophecy often begins to shade into the next three manifestations.

Prophecy can also be a common occurrence. It is less effective when the person on the receiving end is told, "Thus says the Lord." It is more effective when the one prophesying leads with, "When I saw you, I felt that . . ." or "When you said that, I thought . . ." Prophecy works very effectively in daily conversation when the receiver feels that something fairly momentous has been said and is thankful, often teary.

There are many stories among those who practice prophecy about how average people, from store clerks and neighbors to complete strangers, are reduced to tears or have their jaws drop as kind and powerful words are spoken to them in gentle, open-handed ways by a stranger.

Prophecy can be taught, and an exercise in the next chapter has proven very effective in so doing. There is much more on these in the next chapter.

Group 2—*Knowing: Verifiable Revelation*

The next set of three manifestations (word of knowledge, discerning of spirits, and word of wisdom) have a common thread: verifiable revelation. These three manifestations require us to hear specifically and with faith. They do not require spiritual maturity in terms of character, but they do require a willingness and faith to hear in the spirit world and speak what is heard. I have seen instances when a child says something, and an adult's head snaps around to hear the words.

In each case, the person speaking is giving information that can be independently verified. The speaker refers to some fact not fully known to his or her conscious mind but is known to the Holy Spirit. The speaker may not completely understand the meaning of what he or she has said. The thought might come fully formed, or it may be somewhat hidden, like prophecy. The first few words may be given with an urge to speak, or the message may come as a picture or other mental impression. These words can come in a large variety of ways.

The "word of knowledge" reveals a fact or truthful insight that the person does not know "in the natural"—meaning, not having come by it through normal means (hearing others, reading it, etc.). "Distinguishing of spirits" reveals the hidden spiritual source of something: human, God, or demonic—and often the type of spirit. It may give a sense of the purpose behind the words, warning of manipulation or untruth, or a godly "certification" that this is from God. The "word of wisdom" reveals information about God's design and plan, or it gives deep insight into some problem or topic. That insight brings relief, resolution, direction, or some other positive outcome. It was the word, along with a word of knowledge, that was spoken by a stranger to my friend Derri (in the previous chapter) that inspired and guided her when things felt hard, as was God's intention with it.

The Group 1 experience might be very helpful in learning how to begin operating in Group 2. Having humility and holding what is given with an open hand for others to assess is, by far, the best way to approach in Group 2. One of the biggest mistakes in this tier is to keep talking after God has stopped. That mistake is often driven by a sense of wanting to appear more spiritual or mature, or to explain your understanding of what has been said. Best to stop and then say something like, "When I heard that, inside my own understanding, for your consideration is . . ." As was stated at the beginning of this chapter, when we conflate our own identity and reputation with the manifestation, bad things always happen.

Group 3—Doing: Physically Observed Events

The next three take manifestations to a different dynamic. Gifts of healings, miracles, and faith all result in having an impact on something in the physical world that is changed by the spiritual world. We can also call it an overruling or rearranging of the laws of nature. They require a faith-filled action on the part of the believer to move, pray, or do something else in response to the prompting of God that results in the perceptual and physical intervention of God.

Before you decide that this is out of your league, remember that Group 3 is not like getting an advanced degree. The groups are simply to help us understand the nature of the manifestations and not their difficulty in attaining. I have seen brand-new Christians pray for someone, and they are healed. Maybe that is the point—simple, uncomplicated, obedient, childlike faith.

These manifestations can happen in all sorts of ways and promptings, and any explanation or example runs the risk of creating a standard approach. There is none. Jesus put mud in blind eyes, touched others, and simply spoke to others—probably by the leading of the Spirit. You may receive a sense that you are to go to a neighbor and pray for them to be healed. You might feel direction to pray with absolute surety that God will change a certain situation or that He will work a miracle. More often than not, especially when we first enter these manifestations, we will go with some uncertainty and simply try to obey God. We must perform the action at His prompting and leave the results to Him.

We don't declare the results, but we simply ask the person in need if we may pray for them. It requires a willingness to take a risk and to speak and work in deep humility with respect for others. Recall that it is always the work of God through a human, His power, and only at His clear prompting. And we don't need to say, "God told me . . ." to obey God—we simply obey God. Sometimes, acting in a showy or hyperspiritual way turns the recipient completely off and leads to an atmosphere of unbelief.

Manifestations of the Spirit: Understanding the Balance

In numerous discussions about manifestations in general, and specific ones in particular, a few questions (or objections) often come up among more conservative expressions of Christ's Body. They tend to revolve around their opinions or experiences regarding the showy and seemingly useless nature of the manifestations and the harm to those who have suffered from such misuse. Such thoughts have, in turn, fed into the idea that, since this cannot be what God had in mind, then maybe the manifestations themselves, as now portrayed, have ceased. When we search Scripture with this end in mind, we can usually find a pathway to prove our point.

I am not, however, willing to state that both clear and simple scriptural interpretation as well as six hundred million Christians are wrong and are misusing something that has died out. I would have to deny my own long experience in seeing the bad and misuse, and, more importantly, the powerful and undeniable work of God. Paul, in 1 Corinthians 12–14, chastises the Church for just such misuse. They claimed God told them Jesus was accursed, they were speaking over each other to obtain recognition, and they were being showy and shallow. But notice that he calls them to maturity, not to cessation. If there is a false, there must be a true that the false is mimicking.

So to understand what Christ meant and to avoid misuse of manifestations, we need to ask ourselves what maturity looks like.

Paul encouraged Timothy to stir into flame the gift package within him. He states a deep and simple truth: "For God has not given us a spirit of timidity, but of power and love and discipline" (2 Timothy 1:7). In one sentence, the Holy Spirit, through Paul, describes the character and functional approach of the Holy Spirit within each of us as a balance of three things: power, love, and a sound mind. The words for power and love are the common *dunamis* (dynamite!) and *agape* (selfless love). The word translated here as "discipline" is derived from *sophron,* which is a combination of sound thinking, moderation, discretion, and self-discipline all rolled into one.

These three terms are powerful keys to properly understand and use the manifestations of the Holy Spirit—and in understanding the Holy Spirit generally. How so? A tripod is the stand of choice for a steady camera, for survey equipment, and for an easel to enable the creation of a beautiful landscape painting. It is sturdy, adjustable, and simple. Each leg is counterbalanced by the other two. It is constrained by physics to be sturdy in every direction. No matter the slope and unevenness of the ground surface, the camera or theodolite will be sturdy and level through a simple adjustment. It can spin in a 360-degree arc and remain level. The legs can change in length to meet the situation at hand—almost any situation.

We each view the spirit (*pneumatikos*) world and manifestations of the Spirit through our own personal camera lens mounted on our own particular tripod. We have become accustomed to our view(s) of things through that lens. It defines our paradigm—all we know and consider to be true and all we know and consider to be false. If any appearance of a manifestation is not in our paradigm, it may as well not exist. It does not exist for us.

The "true" things (in our view) seem normal, right, and proper. If one of our three spirit-legs is shorter than the others, we have little way of knowing. It is our own lens, after all. And we, as a group or certain expression of the Church, having been together and perhaps somewhat isolated, may unwittingly have a case of "short-leg syndrome." We have become indoctrinated to it—but worse, used to it. It seems normal, right, and comfortable. And we may not be aware or willing to admit that the legs are adjustable. Paul, for example, talks about a last-days church setting where the ungodly members are "holding to a form of godliness although they have denied its power" (2 Timothy 3:5).

If we encounter someone who has a different short-leg syndrome, or even with all three legs the same length, it is hard to see eye-to-eye. They seem unbalanced to us, wrong somehow. And what if we encounter someone, a teaching, or a denomination that has an opposite leg that is shorter or longer than ours? The difference in views is exaggerated. Perhaps their power leg is long and loud while mine is short and mostly ignored. My disciplined thinking leg is proudly and exegetically long, while theirs is short by comparison. We scare each other, avoid each other, ignore each other. You can imagine the problems that brings about in the handicapped-by-man Body of Christ. Many of us don't need to imagine. Sadly, it has been our experience. We teach and live our view, transmitting it to our children. It is rarely questioned—in polite company.

Welcome to denominational perspectives on the Holy Spirit and His gifts!

But what Paul says that the Holy Spirit is in totality, and His gift package in particular (in context here), is a balance of power, love, and a sound mind. A balance. Three legs.

I, more than most, have traveled among the various "lengths-of-legs" organizations for more than forty years. I have been called out on my "leg problems" more than once. Because I did not know at that time about this truth, I was insensitive to the differences and concerns. I can say with the authority of sad experience that this idea, properly applied, would go a long way in filling in what is missing in the Spirit walk of so many in the Church. It certainly did mine. I have come to more admire someone who has three short legs but is in balance than someone who has a very long leg but who has to tilt the world around himself to make it seem level.

It is interesting that Paul's next discussion topic, after his listing of the manifestations, is about the Body being composed of many members (see 1 Corinthians 12:12–26). He states that no part should think less or more of itself in comparison to another. We are to treat the ones the world might deem less honorable with more honor. We need each other to bring us into balance. God has made the Body members each a bit different from others to make us see the need for balance that He designed (see 1 Corinthians 12:24–25). May we bring this desired balance!

1 Corinthians 12–14

So in the genius of Scripture, Paul takes the next three chapters of 1 Corinthians to lay out a power/love/sound mind discussion of the manifestations of the Spirit to help the Corinthians (and us) find the needed balance correction.

First Corinthians 12 is all about the "power" leg. It lays out the overall structure of the grace package, lists the manifestations, gives the body context of the importance of each individual, and then ends with the many-sided grace package each possesses.

First Corinthians 13 may be the most famous Bible chapter in all of Scripture. It is a rebuttal of the heart condition of the church in Corinth, and it is a strong reminder that God is love and love is what binds us all together. It states that a person can exhibit all sorts of manifestations, but without this aspect of the Spirit, it is meaningless—less than meaningless. It ends with a discussion of the temporal nature of all manifestations and the permanent nature of love. In the middle is the description of God's *agape* love (that was read in eighty percent of all 1980s weddings).

In 1 Corinthians 14, Paul lays out practical, detailed, and systematic instructions concerning the two most common manifestations, as well as the two that seem to be most used at will: tongues and prophecy. He gives keys to understanding their nature and use that we will cover in the next chapter. But his major point is that these manifestations are subject to our self-control, and there is nothing unspiritual about that. In fact, the participation of our soul (mind, will, and emotions) is superior to its nonparticipation when in public.

In summary, there are three balancing aspects of the Holy Spirit, and none is superior to the others. Each has a time and a place where it must step up and provide Holy Spirit influence. That balance is of the Spirit, not induced by crazy Pentecostals, not forced by legalistic denominationalists, and not dreamed up by drugged-up free-love hippies. Not that those things might not be present, but they do not preclude the Spirit from bringing balance.

Got it?

The Diagram Continued

Before we move into the next chapter and look at tongues and prophecy, let's look at an updated version of the diagram. You can now see that Paul's analysis extends manifestations to the next Level 3 subcategory—the nine manifestations of the Holy Spirit. That then completes the diagram illustrative of Paul's *pneumatikos* discussion.

Okay. Let's move on to discuss in some detail tongues and prophecy—both the problem in Corinth and, probably, the first two manifestations you have, or will, encounter if you invite the manifestations into your life.

The Spiritual Gifts Blueprint

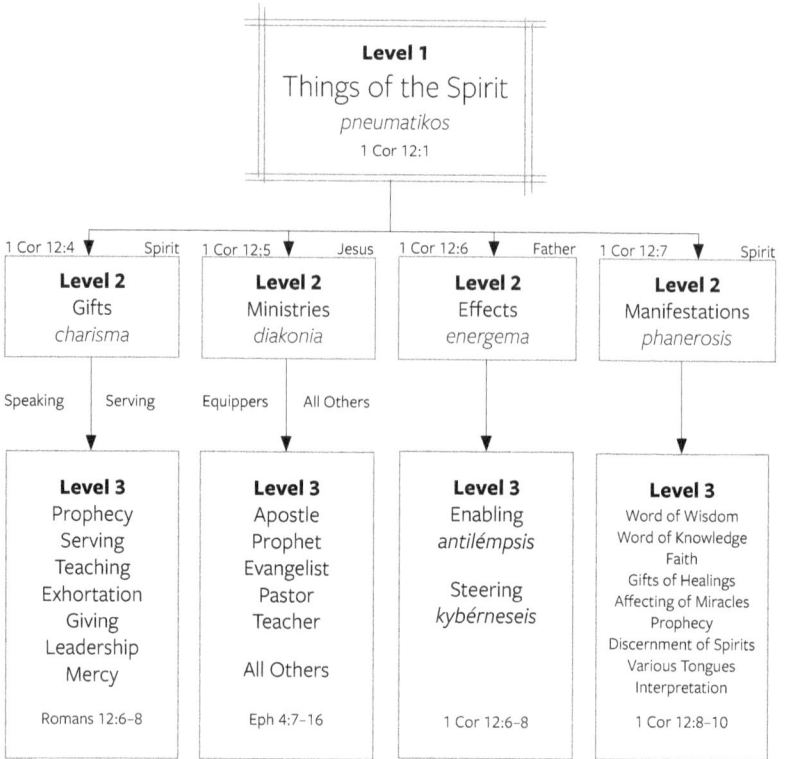

Level 1
Things of the Spirit
pneumatikos
1 Cor 12:1

1 Cor 12:4 ▼ Spirit	1 Cor 12:5 ▼ Jesus	1 Cor 12:6 ▼ Father	1 Cor 12:7 ▼ Spirit
Level 2 Gifts *charisma*	**Level 2** Ministries *diakonia*	**Level 2** Effects *energema*	**Level 2** Manifestations *phanerosis*

Speaking   Serving   Equippers   All Others

Level 3	**Level 3**	**Level 3**	**Level 3**
Prophecy Serving Teaching Exhortation Giving Leadership Mercy	Apostle Prophet Evangelist Pastor Teacher All Others	Enabling *antilémpsis* Steering *kybérneseis*	Word of Wisdom Word of Knowledge Faith Gifts of Healings Affecting of Miracles Prophecy Discernment of Spirits Various Tongues Interpretation
Romans 12:6–8	Eph 4:7–16	1 Cor 12:6–8	1 Cor 12:8–10

Tongues and Prophecy

Overview

Recall that this book is about the four-part spirit structure (*pneumatikos*) articulated by Paul in response to Corinthian questions. Those four parts are gifts (*charisma*), ministries (*diakonia*), effects (*energema*), and the topic of the last chapter and this one, manifestations of the Holy Spirit (*phanerosis*).

In the last chapter, I laid out an overview and detailed discussion of the nine manifestations of the Holy Spirit as articulated by Paul (see 1 Corinthians 12:7–11). In this chapter, I want to talk specifically about tongues and prophecy. As mentioned, this discussion is important, as these two manifestations often serve as a basis or proving ground for future use of the other manifestations. If you get these two right, the others follow along much more comfortably. Here is a summary of the basics of what Paul says to the Corinthians about these two in terms of his desire for their proper use by them and, by extension, any church.

Now I wish that you all spoke in tongues, but rather that you would prophesy. . . . I thank God, I speak in tongues more than you all. . . .

For you can all prophesy one by one, so that all may learn and all may be exhorted. . . . Therefore, my brothers and sisters, earnestly desire to prophesy, and do not forbid speaking in tongues. But all things must be done properly and in an orderly way.

1 Corinthians 14:5, 18, 31, 39–40

While all manifestations can feel edgy, historically these two—tongues and prophecy—have caused misunderstandings and concerns. This may be because of both their apparent strangeness and commonality. Perhaps the largest schism within the Church today is not Catholic and Protestant, but Pentecostal/charismatic and . . . well, whatever the other title should be.

Over the last forty-plus years, I have been involved in some form of leadership with about twenty different groups, churches, and Bible studies. Each struggled with these concepts, especially at the onset of the Charismatic Movement in the 1970s. Much of that struggle continues, though it is more muted, and most churches and denominations are simply set in the ways of any previous decision by leaders that was articulated or tacitly adopted.

But, on the other hand, proper use of these two manifestations has changed countless lives for the better. They often trigger a sense of living with an active Holy Spirit with whom they can commune. This was Paul's point exactly when he described the connected nature of the four-part structure of things of the spirit. Among my more conservative Christian relationships, I am seeing an increasing interest in or curiosity about these phenomena and a wary but growing acceptance of them when practiced unobtrusively.

Having dwelt comfortably within both "camps," I would like to offer some insight into tongues and prophecy in the hope that it will help give a clearer picture of their value without exaggeration or misplaced emphasis. Please keep in mind the three-part "balance" discussion from the previous chapter.

Before we move to tongues, we need to understand something about us. It's important—trust me.

Man's Makeup

Foundational to understanding both the purposes of these two manifestations and how they operate is understanding man's makeup. There are differing views. Anthropological monism says we are one thing—a human. And that is right. Dichotomism says we humans are body and soul. It says that when we die, our body falls to the ground and the soul goes to God. And that, too, is right. But from an operational view, trichotomism says we are three parts. Paul is coming from this perspective when he says, "Now may the God of peace Himself sanctify you entirely; and may your spirit and soul and body be kept complete, without blame at the coming of our Lord Jesus Christ" (1 Thessalonians 5:23). He uses three words, in that order, to describe our makeup: spirit (*pneuma*), soul (*psyche*), and body (*soma*). Jesus refers to this makeup as quoted and explained by John.

> "The one who believes in Me, as the Scripture said, 'From his innermost being will flow rivers of living water.'" But this He said in reference to the Spirit, whom those who believed in Him were to receive; for the Spirit was not yet given, because Jesus was not yet glorified.
>
> John 7:38–39

From our innermost part, our human spirit, there will be a continuous flow of the Holy Spirit. When Jesus was glorified, the Father sent the Holy Spirit upon and into those in the Upper Room and the flow began. And part of that flow was expressed in tongues and prophecy out of the mouths of the newly filled. While this happened several times in Acts, it has been repeated hundreds of times in history. It is still true today, as demonstrated by hundreds of millions of people. There is a flow that comes out of my spirit, through my soul, out of my mouth, and into the world. And one of the ways that flow is expressed is in the form of tongues and prophecy. The book *Like a Mighty Wind* by Mel Tari and Cliff Dudley is a Christian classic that provides an amazing account of this happening on the island of Timor in 1965.[1]

Why is understanding this flow and our makeup important? Paul describes three kinds of men on the basis of primary motivation.

These three refer to the three parts of man described above: the flesh (body-driven) man, the natural (soulish) man, and the spiritual man:

> And I, brothers and sisters, could not speak to you as spiritual [*pneumatikos*] people, but only as fleshly, as to infants in Christ. I gave you milk to drink, not solid food; for you were not yet able to consume it. But even now you are not yet able, for you are still fleshly [*sarkikos*]. For since there is jealousy and strife among you, are you not fleshly, and are you not walking like ordinary people?
>
> 1 Corinthians 3:1–3

> But a natural [*psychikos*] person does not accept the things of the Spirit of God, for they are foolishness to him; and he cannot understand them, because they are spiritually discerned. But the one who is spiritual [*pneumatikos*] discerns all things, yet he himself is discerned by no one.
>
> 1 Corinthians 2:14–15

While we would all agree that the flesh (*sarkikos*) man, being driven by physical emotions and drives, is not humanity's highest and best, Paul makes a further distinction in these verses, saying that the natural (mind-will-emotions, *psychikos*) man cannot rightly appraise the spiritual (*pneumatikos*) man nor things of the spirit. They appear foolish to him.

In much of the Western Church, we highly prize deep intellectual understanding of Scripture and erudite preaching and teaching. Thousands of theses and books have been written on proper hermeneutical understanding and sound exegesis of minute portions of Scripture—the purview of the soul man. Yet, by comparison, scant attention has been paid to the immense value of real-time connection with the members of the Trinity and walking and living in the four-part spirit structure—including tongues and prophecy. It seems foolish, and some churches demonstrate a Corinthian lack of maturity in their use that seems to prove their foolishness. Yet these two manifestations often serve as a foundation of the spiritual man, however poorly occupied and represented it is.

So here is a foundational understanding. My spirit is the head of my being and the dwelling place of the Trinity. My soul is the steward that is carrying out the desires of my spirit and the Holy Spirit living within. My body is the slave that is kept healthy and under control—obeying direction. I am to learn to live "out from" my spirit—to become that spiritual man. I find that hard to do because my soul (mind, will, and emotions) has held supremacy my whole life.

How then do I make the transition to a spirit/Spirit-led life and lifestyle? What tools are there to help me exercise that capability and give my spirit supremacy both within me and out of me? Oh, the wisdom of God. "The foolishness of God is wiser than mankind, and the weakness of God is stronger than mankind" (1 Corinthians 1:25). Two very effective, God-provided ways (that sometimes appear foolish) for this to be learned are through the practice of tongues and prophecy. They help to accomplish the job of transitioning us into being much more "spiritual" (i.e., *pneumatikos* people) in ways like nothing else can.

Let's now turn to the question that many have asked in the past couple hundred years, "Didn't these manifestations die out long ago?" Not at all.

Manifestations through the Ages

History shows us that since the Day of Pentecost, a group of people somewhere has always practiced speaking in tongues and prophecy.[2] Because speaking in tongues is easier than prophecy to track historically, let's briefly follow that path, realizing that other manifestations tended to follow speaking in tongues.

Speaking in tongues (and prophecy) was fairly common in the early Church. According to Irenaeus,

> In like manner we do also hear many brethren in the Church who possess prophetic gifts and who through the Spirit speak all kinds of languages, and bring to light for the general benefit the hidden things of men, and declare the mysteries of God.[3]

Early Church history tells us that many of the early Church leaders, including Tertullian, Origen, and Novatian, were well acquainted with and supportive of both tongues and prophecy, with such evidence being clear through the end of the second century.

Manifestations of the Spirit began to decline as formalism grew within the Church. By the medieval time period, most Church authorities declared that the practice of tongues was no longer possible or available. They declared this was only a manifestation available to the early apostles, and perhaps, those who were connected directly with them.

Others felt differently, thinking that the Church had taken a wrong turn, not the manifestations. Various groups such as the French Camisards, Montanists,* Jansenists, and Waldensians continued believing in the practice of tongues. A number of monastics, including the likes of Francis of Assisi, also exhibited various manifestations. The Shakers, who thrived from about 1837 to 1847, spoke in tongues including hymns and prayers. The Quakers, the early Methodists, and some Presbyterians also spoke in tongues.

The early Churches of Christ and Christian Church movements grew out of the Cane Ridge Revival of 1801, which included numerous manifestations and experiences, including speaking in tongues. Tongues experienced a resurgence at the beginning of the twentieth century through the Azusa Street Revival that started the Pentecostal Movement. The subsequent Charismatic Renewal in the 1960s and 1970s spread the manifestation among a new generation who stepped back from the mandate of tongues as the demonstration of being "baptized in the Holy Spirit" expressed by Pentecostalism. It has been estimated that about 600 million Christians worldwide probably practice glossolalia (tongues).[4]

With that overview of the long and sometimes thin chain linking Pentecost and today, let's turn to tongues.

---

*Montanus is a good example of the difficulties. While he exhibited a blameless life and doctrine, his focus on the soon Second Coming of Christ and emphasis on spiritual manifestations brought him under suspicion.

More on Tongues

Tongues is the ability to speak and pray out of our spirit in a language we do not know, perhaps (but not exclusively) in a language no one on earth knows. This happens in a manner in which the conscious mind plays little or no part.

A Summary of Paul's Teachings on Tongues

Most of us know about the appearance of tongues and prophecy in the book of Acts. But what about the ongoing use of tongues? Paul, in 1 Corinthians 14 in a discussion that is generally negative concerning the Corinthian use of tongues, says a lot of mostly positive things about the manifestation, and he gives guidance in its use.

Facts about tongues:

- You speak mysteries to God, not men, within your spirit (verse 2).
- You build yourself up—edify yourself (verse 4).
- Paul wishes all spoke in tongues, implying it would be a good and maybe even a possible thing, and tongues plus interpretation is the equivalent of prophecy (verse 5).
- It is not gibberish—if the visible practice is the actual manifestation, then it has meaning (verse 10).
- You are to pray that you interpret when you speak in a tongue publicly for the purpose of edification (verse 13).
- Your spirit prays when you pray in a tongue, but your mind is unfruitful or uninvolved—not in control (verse 14).
- You can pray, sing, bless, and give thanks in tongues (verses 15–17).
- Tongues, used appropriately in the right setting, can also be a sign to unbelievers† (verse 22).

---

†Experience from trustworthy sources and anecdotal reporting elsewhere illustrates that it can take on a different form where the hearer can tell what is being said even when the speaker is not sure. Pentecost was an example of this

Guidance on the proper use of tongues:

- The use of tongues repeatedly or together without an interpreter or interpretation will be chaotic and unfruitful for the unbeliever or the one not knowledgeable about manifestations* (verse 23).
- All things have the end goal of edifying (building up) the local body. If that is not the outcome, then the activities are to stop (verse 26).
- Two or three tongues ought to be enough to give the sense of a word needing interpretation (verse 27).
- Don't speak out loud if no one with known ability in interpretation is present; it is fruitful and acceptable to pray to yourself (e.g., under your breath, quietly) and to God (verse 28).
- Do not forbid tongue speaking (verse 39).

Paul also says to the Corinthians that if they are not sufficiently careful about spiritual influences, it may have an impact on their meetings. Someone said, "Jesus is accursed" in a meeting moved by "the spirit." Paul says that is rubbish (see 1 Corinthians 12:3). John says a similar thing concerning not believing every spiritual influence that comes to you—but test the spirits (see 1 John 4:1–2). In neither case do Paul or John say that we are to withdraw from listening to the spirit side of things. They do, however, instruct us to simply use more wise discernment and judgment.

Is all this talk about tongues hogwash, as some have said? Well . . .

---

form of tongues, although the miracle might have been in the hearing, since they *each* heard *them* speaking in their native dialect (see Acts 2:6).

*One might consider some of the unhelpful fruit of various Pentecostal expressions here. Though some of the most uplifting times of worship I have experienced have been in foreign countries where all praised God at once (no attempt at communicating with each other, only with God) and it was clear to me some were praising in their own language, and some were simply praising in tongues. In both cases, it seemed perfectly acceptable. The fruitful outcome is the point.

Scientific Evidence

Many scientific studies or demonstrations exist that help frame our understanding of what tongues actually is. Let's take a quick objective look at some of the evidence.

The idea that, as Paul says, the "mind is unfruitful" (1 Corinthians 14:14 NIV) has been demonstrated with brain scans. For example, Dr. Andrew B. Newberg from the University of Pennsylvania, and others, has used single photon emission computer tomography (SPECT) scans of people praying normally and then in tongues, and found that there were specific and distinctive differences observed in the switch. Newberg is quoted as saying that the most important difference between the two types of prayer was a marked decrease in frontal lobe function. He says, "The part of the brain that normally makes them feel in control has been essentially shut down."[5] Or as Paul put it, "My mind is unfruitful" (1 Corinthians 14:14 NIV). Interestingly, in a Johns Hopkins study of jazz musicians improvising, somewhat similar types of brain scan differences were found— a slowdown of function within the dorsolateral prefrontal cortex.[6]

A study of 990 male evangelical clergy in England found that those who engaged in the practice of tongues were more correlated with stable extroversion and negatively with neuroticism, and tongues was unrelated to psychoticism.[7]

Non-Christians speak in tongues. In her cross-cultural study, Felicitas D. Goodman describes the use of "tongues" by various cultures and religions, and states that Christians have this "quaint" view that it is limited to Christians and mostly to the first century of the Christian Church.[8]

Goodman also stated that it was clear that glossolalia can be a learned behavior. Another researcher stated, "Glossolalia research has convinced me that it is a learned behavior which can bring a sense of power and well-being."[9] An experiment conducted in a non-spiritual setting had participants listen to a recorded sample of genuine glossolalia. After listening to the recording, twenty percent of the subjects were able to mimic the sounds and "speak in tongues" immediately. Further, after some coaching, seventy percent of the subjects were able to speak in some form of glossolalia, however haltingly. The conclusion to the study was that "Glossolalia, therefore, seems likely to be a type of learned behavior rather than a special altered state of mind."[10] A young female YouTube sensation received over twenty million views speaking a semi-impromptu flowing gibberish but with perfect accents sounding like twenty different languages.[11]

Conclusions about Tongues

What are we to make of all this? I personally have come to a set of conclusions that balance research, Scripture, and a wide range of experiences from hundreds of situations in my own life and in the lives of others:

1. The ability to speak in tongues, or gibberish, is a subset of a human ability that is easily accessed by some to "flow" in various creative expressions, be they speech or music. This is done through partially bypassing certain parts of the brain related to cognitive processing and to "intuit" the outflow. Glossolalia can be a learned behavior rather than always being a spontaneous outburst. That does not negate the idea that it can also be supernatural.

2. The Holy Spirit dwelling within the human spirit uses this innate human ability of the soul to allow the "river" spoken of by Christ to flow out from the human spirit through many expressions of speech and song.

3. A person can be taught to take advantage of this human capability to "speak in tongues." If a person begins to release that flow and turns inward asking God to speak from within them, the flow normally shifts from being initially somewhat halting (because the mind is demanding to understand and control) to beginning to flow naturally, like an artesian spring being unclogged.

4. This flow is controllable by the will of the person; although, just as strong emotion is not always fully controlled,

neither is this flow always fully controlled. There can be ecstatic outbursts in tongues during worship, sometimes accompanied by strong emotions.

5. This flow does many things among people, which includes allowing the person to begin to learn to better perceive the sources within themselves of inspiration, to understand the difference between the soul's voice and that of the spirit, to give thanks well, to pray with specific exactitude the will of God in a specific situation, and to help train the human soul to better take a "stewardship" position in that tripartite makeup of a human.

6. Tongues as a supernatural manifestation is not limited to Christian use but can be copied and used by Satan to imbue his subjects with a sense of power and mysticism. It is a spirit (God's, mine, or demonic) using the soul/body to bring sound out of the mouth. The fact that it can be counterfeited does not mean it is false. On the contrary, the good fruit of tongues, when practiced biblically, and the fact it is counterfeited, might more strongly imply its authenticity.

Application Summary and My Story

Can you learn to speak in tongues? The evidence above seems to imply you can. That has been my experience in my own life and in the lives of many others I know. One of the best ways I know is how I was led into tongues as a two-week-old Christian. Without getting into details, I was a bit sad and frustrated at a failed witnessing attempt, sitting on a log in the woods by a picnic area. Two young men came walking up the path, asked me about my sadness, chatted for a minute, and then sat down on the log on either side of me. They spoke encouragement to me and asked if I had ever asked the Holy Spirit to fill me. Like in Ephesus in Acts 19:2, I responded that I had not heard of that. They led me in a prayer in which I asked the Holy Spirit to fill me, and they encouraged me to speak words of worship and gratitude to the Lord. One of them said, "When English seems too slow and clumsy, keep speaking but forget about forming words. Just speak out whatever comes up."

We prayed together. The one on my right began to speak in what I now know was tongues. As joy overflowed in me, my vocabulary fell short of what I wanted to exclaim. I accepted the invitation, and I simply began to let out sounds, not words. I did not mimic him, but his own tongues encouraged me. I saw the technique.

Well, then things got interesting. Within about a minute, I was excitedly praising in a language I had never heard. I stopped, and they smiled and encouraged me to keep going. After about ten minutes, they walked back into the woods. I never saw them again, but my life was changed as the door to manifestations was opened. I'm pretty sure they were not angels—right?

Since that time, I have experienced tongues in various public and private settings—sometimes interceding intensely with two or three others for something. One time I was in Germany with a group of about seven hundred people from all over Europe. In the midst of a praise song, the leader simply began to praise God in German. This leader encouraged all of us to praise Him in our native tongue. The seven hundred people each began to praise Him in their own tongue. I'm sure I heard French, Italian, Greek, and—well, tongues. It was resoundingly awesome, and it reminded me of the great praise throng mentioned in Revelation 7:9–12. (I encourage you to read this passage if you don't know what I'm talking about.)

Another time, I was traveling with several people across the desert at night, returning to our university in Colorado. Someone asked me about tongues, and I explained as best I could. A young woman in the back seat said, "Stop. I want to do that right now!" We pulled over, and after a bit of explanation (like the two young men gave me), she burst out with a fluting song. We were sitting under a full moon next to a cactus tree, and her song was answered by coyotes! I told her it wasn't always like that. She just smiled. It might be always like that for her!

I pray in tongues almost daily. I do it when I'm mowing, hiking, facing a problem, feeling bored, needing inner encouragement, or when I'm not sure what to write next about tongues! A mentor of mine bursts into tongues when he is facing temptation, stating it gives him leverage that soulish prayer does not to counteract the temptation of the devil, and to "by the Spirit . . . [put] to death the deeds of the body" (Romans 8:13). It's a very useful multitool. Paul says it is also useful in a church assembly, if done properly. I'd not start there. Just saying.

What are some helpful steps to begin speaking in tongues? Using some of the conclusions above as a brief preteaching, I have led people into tongues. Here are four simple steps that were used for me and that I have passed on to others:

1. Settle your heart and mind and ask God's Spirit to fill you for His purposes and the purpose of praise.
2. Begin to envision Him in His glory and praise Him without self-consciousness.
3. When brain-formed words seem like they are not enough, simply (and non-self-consciously) let the river flow.
4. It may trickle at first, but don't stop! Stay with it for at least five or ten minutes.

Then return to it often. During the next few weeks, it will stabilize and become more and more uplifting. Keep this practice to yourself for a while. Let your consciousness of the flow gain ascendency in your life. It may, over time, take on different-sounding languages depending on whether you sense you are praying for specific things or if you are simply praising. Mine does. See if Paul isn't right.

Don't be afraid.

Let's now turn to New Testament prophecy.

Prophecy—What Is It?

As Paul summarizes in 1 Corinthians 14:3, "The one who prophesies speaks to people for their upbuilding and encouragement and consolation" (ESV). New Testament prophecy is for everyone, not just a few (see 1 Corinthians 14:5), and, I have come to believe, its best use is outside of a church setting when people least expect to sense the warm love of God spoken by a normal person. It is the life blood of the Church—and of relationships of all types. It is one of God's main means of spreading personal encouragement to every part of the Body. It is nonoptional. And He trusts us to do it.

An Overview of Using Prophecy

Every pastor and teacher hopes that what they have to say is inspired by God. Every friend in an Ephesians 4 ligament relationship (see chapter 5 for a definition) hopes to be able to speak more than just nice words to their friends. We hope to bring the things God wants to say to those we love. We each secretly hope that someone can really see us and that they will encourage us and praise us for what they see. The description of ligament relationships in chapter 5 sounds so good—but how can it be? Prophecy is a big part of God's answer to these legitimate needs and desires.

Yet perhaps because our picture of being prophetic seems either terribly showy or terribly intimidating, we place the whole idea in our "too hard" box and move along. We fail to realize that God wishes to speak both to us and through us, and He wants us to purpose to learn His ways and His voice. He wishes we would discover that being prophetic has nothing to do with being deep, scary, and "woo-woo." It has, instead, everything to do with being a simple and faithful messenger and friend.

Manifestations of prophecy in the New Testament differ from the Old Testament version, where it was expected that the uniquely Spirit-filled prophet spoke the infallible Word of God, judged Israel, and often foretold the future. We might think of them as "capital P prophets."

Also recall that there is a *charisma* gift of prophecy in the New Testament, as well as the five-fold office of being a Prophet (another capital P). Although giving words of prophecy is the specific focus of those who hold this office, and God gives them special ability to fill that role, every Christian is called to speak to others the goodness and kindness of God; therefore, all who do that are also prophesying!

Let's look at other ways prophecy is different in the New Testament from the Old Testament. First of all, as discussed in the previous chapter, we are all filled with the Holy Spirit, thus we can all prophesy—any manifestation of the spirit is available to any child of God when faith meets need. The New Testament manifestation of prophecy is not about telling the future or needing to share specific things that were revealed supernaturally (that is a word of knowledge). Paul says that prophecy is gentle revelation given by God through another person for the three general purposes (see 1 Corinthians 14:3).

- Edification, Upbuilding (*oikedome*—the "family house"). Words that build up the family house, that build up and strengthen, that encourage, and that make stronger.
- Encouragement (*paraklesis*—"call alongside"). Running beside someone giving them strong encouragement to keep them going, urging them to be their best, telling them they will make it and that they are not alone, and bringing uplifting truth along the way. Recall the description of the marathon runner in chapter 4 with the designated *parakaleo* running the last stretch calling encouragement. It is that.
- Consolation and Comfort (*paramuthia*—"whisper sweetly and lovingly in the ear"). It is speaking intimately and sweetly of love, care, and tenderness, and pouring healing oil into the soul. It is allowing the Comforter (Holy Spirit) to comfort through us.

Prophecy expresses "God's compliment" to another person. It can be deep, meaningful, and inspiring. But the language does not need to sound Shakespearian, poetic, or lyrical. It is simple, heartfelt words that somehow carry the power of God within them. Prophecy offers encouragement with the power and authority not contained in just "being nice." It often shades toward words of knowledge in which the words spoken carry great meaning to the hearer but are unknown to the speaker.

173

Here are a few examples. Notice the wording, and the giving with an open hand and without a "God told me" mandate.

I was speaking in Romania on this topic with the aid of a young female translator. The church I was presenting to was filled with young people. I wanted to demonstrate the idea that we just speak in plain Engli . . . er, Romanian. To illustrate what that might sound like, I turned to my translator and said, "Sweetie Bear, you are God's chosen instrument to help spread the idea that this gift is for everyone." She tried to speak and then simply broke down crying.

When she caught her breath she said, "That name, Sweetie Bear, is the name my dear grandfather called me. He was my mentor." I was the most surprised—I had no idea. God did. God does things like this to grab the attention of the hearer and to bring about the intended result more forcefully. A ripple of wonder went through the audience, and by the end of the day, they had all learned to prophesy. They even asked if they "could take it to the streets." I answered, "Preferably." They did.

A store clerk was working feverishly to reduce the long checkout line. I looked at her and the Spirit quietly asked me to notice her. I saw her heart. And when I got to the front I simply said, "You are an amazing and responsible young woman in a tough job. You are doing so well, and God has great things in store for you. Don't worry." She stared for about two seconds and then burst into tears, apologizing. She came around the counter and hugged me saying, "You just made my whole week. Thank you so much."

A councilman was in a tough situation trying to do the right thing, the honest thing, but he was surrounded by corruption. I watched him in the meeting in which I presented. Afterward, after the press and others were gone, I approached him. He looked tired, as if he was thinking, *Now what?* I heard, and I told him, "Your honesty and desire for fairness is so refreshing. I wanted to encourage you that I think God loves that about you." Tears trickled down his cheeks. With a "thank you," we exchanged business cards and have remained long-term friends.

A fireball leader was building relationships in many countries, bringing connection to everyone. Yet she was alone, single, and lonely. As we chatted, the Spirit asked me to hush and simply say to her, "My love, He sees you. He is with you when you are alone at night and when you awake. He tells angels about His girl. And He let me see you for who you really are. He is so proud of you." She looked at me, looked away, and her shoulders shuddered. "No fair!" she said, "Now my mascara is ruined." We hugged. She went her way—not alone.

That is our job. Want in?

Application

In 1 Corinthians 14:1, God, through Paul, says, "Pursue the love, and seek earnestly the spiritual things, and rather that ye may prophecy" (YLT). It is clearly for everyone. Paul speaks of a more orderly Corinthian church environment where everyone is comfortable moving "prophetically"—even needing to take turns—as the Spirit moves among them (see 1 Corinthians 14:24, 30). And this is to continue in the church until Jesus, the "Perfect," returns and "I will know fully, just as I also have been fully known" (1 Corinthians 13:12).

If God's desire for each of us is to prophesy, then it is very possible that when we practice it often, it will become almost natural (in a supernatural way). Our job is to get over our fears of failure (of course, we will make mistakes), our misconceptions that prophecy is some guy in a beard bellowing "thus sayeth the Lord," and our sense that we are not worthy to be used in such a way (since it is not about us, anyway).

The first hurdle is to ensure that each of us knows that we can, and do, hear God. Jesus said that His sheep hear His voice (see John 10:4–5). You are His sheep, so that should be settled. But remember that God is not human, and His first language is not anybody's native tongue. While God often uses external things to communicate to us (nature, signs, Bible verses, coincidences, etc.), His primary means is to speak to us from the inside of us where He lives (see Psalm 32:8).

Earlier, I described the three inner "screens" that each human has and that we pay attention to throughout the day: senses and drives, memory and analysis, imagination and impression. God uses all three screens, but the last one is the most flexible. When we focus on that screen, we can often sense what He is saying. These impressions bubble up on the inside of us from our spirit and may suddenly appear in our mind as a thought or picture, or even as a whole understanding suddenly within us.

We do not have to be afraid. God is far more powerful and more able to give us words that are real than Satan and all his demons are at deceiving us (see Luke 11:9–13). We do not have to be afraid if we are simply asking God to speak through us and not trying, out of fear or pride, to show off. You can be bold (not brash), confident (not arrogant), and gentle (not fearful). God's flow out of the center of us is always able to be accessed (see John 7:38–39).

Personal Application—How to Give a Prophecy

Prophecy is especially effective within the ligament relationships described in chapter 5 when we speak truth in love one to another. We are to be faithful messengers. Paul, in the middle of the "love" chapter (which is 1 Corinthians 13) says that "we know in part and prophesy in part" (verse 9). We push our puzzle piece to the middle and take our hands off of it. Our goal is the same as God's, which is to give grace (God's life and energy) to the hearer and not to grieve the Holy Spirit.

> Let no unwholesome word come out of your mouth, but if there is any good word for edification according to the need of the moment, say that, so that it will give grace to those who hear. Do not grieve the Holy Spirit of God, by whom you were sealed for the day of redemption.
>
> Ephesians 4:29–30

An old prophet once told me, "A young prophet gets a word and blurts it out. An older prophet gets a word and awaits the right time to give it. But the wisest prophets get a word and ask God what He wants done with it—which may include never speaking it."

It is important to understand that some revelation, especially in our prayer life, is given for the purposes of our personal intercession, and we should only share it if, and when, we feel God is prompting us. In a personal ministry setting, many words are to be held to help guide the ministry, and God will speak those things directly to the person being ministered to. We simply make space for that to happen.

God loves to use our style, personality, and way of expression as a channel of His word given to another. He even loves to watch another look on us with astonishment and think we're great. We know the truth: He is great, and we are in love with Him. In my life, I return thanks when I lay down at night and recount the day.

Any spoken revelation has three parts:

1. The Revelation—This is our best and clearest attempt to faithfully and simply convey only what God has said or shown to us that we feel He wants us to convey. We do this without opinions, explanation, or sometimes without even understanding. Above all, we are faithful and simple messengers.

2. The Interpretation—This is a God-led explanation of what has been said, perhaps applied to the person, the situation, or the circumstance. It may explain a symbolic picture or word.

3. The Application—This is what the person should, or might, do in response to the word that has been given.

It is important not to inadvertently merge those three parts together, especially if you are the one giving the first part of the prophecy. I recall a time when my two roommates and I attended a newer church in Denver. A young man stood and began to give a prophetic word. What he began to share was spot on and clearly inspired. But then God stopped, and the young man kept going. Both of my roommates glanced at me with raised eyebrows and subtle smiles. I bet half the congregation knew. The young man was not satisfied that what God spoke had been explained well enough, and he decided to finish the job—sliding into interpretation. On the way home we joked that he should have said, "God said . . . and furthermore . . ."

You will rarely have the interpretation or application. In a ministry setting, it would be biblical to let the person hearing the word first seek God for its meaning. After they have had a chance to hear God, perhaps in the ministry recap, you might suggest the things it meant to you when you heard or saw it from God. Don't worry—God is watching over His word to perform it (see Jeremiah 1:12).

Sometimes things get strange, and the experienced maturity of the prophet makes all the difference. Well-known prophet Bob Jones once spoke to me and said, "Wow, Satan sure has a plan for you." That was all that he said. I pondered for weeks, kept watch, and finally came to the place that I would never, ever, ever give the devil an opportunity to carry out his scheme. I grew strong in that area and became able to observe his schemes in others who were ministering in the Freedom Prayer ministry (mentioned earlier). Years later at a conference, I ran into Bob standing "accidentally" alone. I complained to him about his word to me. He smiled, looked hard into my eyes, nodded, and said, "It worked, didn't it?" That changed everything.

Here are a few final pointers:

- Start simply and allow God to use you without fear. Stop when He stops.
- Don't be directive or manipulative. No "dates, mates, or babies."
- Ask the person if what you said has meaning to them, and don't be defensive.
- Don't say, "Thus sayeth the Lord. . . ." Instead, say things like, "How does this sound to you?" "This thought just came to me," "I feel like God might be saying," "I got this impression that," "When I looked at you, I saw a picture of," "Does this mean anything to you?"
- Give the person a graceful way to say, "No, that doesn't mean anything to me." Often, at a later time, something happens in their life and the word rises up within them to give them wisdom or encouragement at just the right time.

Let's turn now to the other half of the equation, which is how to receive a prophecy.

Personal Application—*How to Receive a Prophecy*

Just as we are not to "grieve the Holy Spirit" (Ephesians 4:30) when we give a prophetic word, we are also told, specifically, not to "quench" the Spirit in the reception of a prophecy:

> Do not quench the Spirit, do not utterly reject prophecies, but examine everything; hold firmly to that which is good, abstain from every form of evil.
>
> 1 Thessalonians 5:19–22

Paul shares several interrelated things about how to receive potentially prophetic words in the above verses. Notice the balance he gives. On the negative side, don't quench the Spirit and don't reject prophetic words. On the positive side, examine everything carefully and hold fast to the good.

The word *quench* can mean the physical quenching of a fire with water, or the metaphorical quenching or stifling of the Holy Spirit. It seems amazing that humans can quench the infinite Holy Spirit as He speaks through an individual—and do so easily. But He is very gentle, and we are insecure. His work in a meeting and in humans seems to be fairly easily quenched through interruption and distraction, an atmosphere of opposition or unbelief, overcontrolled church services, active resistance, or making potentially prophetic words scary and difficult, maybe even unacceptable. Such an atmosphere is a bit like a self-fulfilling prophecy. We create an atmosphere where it cannot happen, and it does not happen. "See! I'm right."

But the balancing answer is not to have a wide-open door where anything goes. We should not, for example, create an environment in which someone can stand up and say, "Jesus is accursed" (see 1 Corinthians 12:3). But, as Paul says, we are to examine or test carefully and hold fast to the good. That word means to think it through in light of scriptural truth and with the thoughts of other mature individuals.

Notice it does not say what to do with the leftovers, the ones that do not pass the test. But I bet encouraging instruction and correction go a long way in helping the inexperienced gain confidence in the Lord, as well as a gentle appreciation of their own fallibility.

God is accurate; humans are not. As with the young man I mentioned earlier who moved into self-interpretation, we must understand that there will often be some level of "missing it," as well as some trial and error—some "know in part and prophesy in part" (1 Corinthians 13:9). Sometimes the word only makes sense later when we see it happening in life—then we are in awe. In the light of that reality, we are to encourage the prophetic with our attitudes. We hold fast and don't let go of that which seems good and seems to carry the stamp of God. And we let the other slide away without judgment or criticism. There may be a time for training or correction later, but not at the time the word is given.

In his letter to the Corinthians, Paul lays out his own sense of orderly prophecy in meetings.

> Have two or three prophets speak, and have the others pass judgment. But if a revelation is made to another who is seated, then the first one is to keep silent. For you can all prophesy one by one, so that all may learn and all may be exhorted; and the spirits of prophets are subject to prophets; for God is not a God of confusion, but of peace.
>
> 1 Corinthians 14:29–33

Some churches have a "prophecy station" where those who feel they have something to say submit it to an elder or mature individual who makes a real-time judgment in terms of whether it should be given now, should be held on to for now, or requires a "let's talk after the meeting" conversation. In smaller house church settings, the more informal self-governing approach of Paul makes more sense.

Those who speak must know that what they say is fair game for examination. That is biblical and godly. When we judge or assess a prophetic word, we must be careful about demanding "scriptural confirmation." This approach has the ring of wisdom, but it also sometimes betrays an arrogant unbelief or an "I know it all" attitude rather than prudence. We are all surprised about how our "right" answers change over time and with experience.

I hope it is obvious, but just in case it is not, I will say it: Prophecy should never contradict the Word of God. Often God will confirm a word He has spoken in other ways, or it may just have a warm and good feeling deep on the inside—like it connects with where we are. Sometimes a Scripture verse that goes with the word will suddenly come to mind.

When we operate with this attitude, we create fertile ground for God to move and for the manifestation of prophecy to grow in power, accuracy, and effect. We foster an atmosphere where everyone feels empowered to hear God and speak His words. Even the youngest do not have a "junior Holy Spirit." They can speak wonderful words.

Prophecy Hot Seat Exercise—Learning How to Prophesy
Introduction

This is a fun and easy exercise to teach people how to better hear God and how to prophesy according to the New Testament definition. I have done this on three continents, in both charismatic and very conservative settings, and the results bring lots of laughter, tears, and head shaking at God's goodness and the ease of prophecy. It is low-pressure, is fun, and always yields interesting results and strong encouragement. It is nonreligious but not irreligious. It takes into account Paul's thoughts in 1 Corinthians 14 that we all prophesy in part—but we all can prophesy.

Recall the "Sweetie Bear" story in Romania? We did this prophecy hot seat exercise there and received a great response. After the third round, when the senior pastor had seen the wonderful things that had begun to happen, he asked if he could be in the "hot seat." He desired "a word." The students said they were "taking this to the streets" and began to excitedly plan how. Now a local Christian school uses this every year at their senior retreat. One of the young men told me years later how much "the cry thing" had impacted his class.

In the United States, some student group members were so excited about this exercise that they decided to practice with each other and then open a booth at a state fair. They called it "Psalm Reading." They shared that many encouraging things happened, and the process sparked many interesting conversations.

There can be some danger in personal prophecy and the abuse of it if there is not a mature and experienced person in the mix and if clear boundaries have not been established. The teaching and exercise are designed to keep things within safe boundaries under church authority. The goal is to begin to get a sense of the flow of the Spirit and of God.

The Exercise

Teach these things in the introduction.

Say, "In a few short minutes, you will prophesy over each other. It will be fun!" Make sure they know that you will not embarrass anyone, but it may be that God will stretch and encourage them. Also let participants know that no one will be forced to do anything, and no one will have to do anything in front of the group.

Remind them of the DNA of godly prophecy. It is gentle and love-filled, not manipulative. No dates, mates, or babies—or anything directive. It is not condemning. They are to ask if something said has meaning rather than demand that the recipient figures something out. They are not interpreting or applying the prophecy before the listeners have had a chance to consider what has been said.

Tell them that if they honestly and humbly ask God a direct question, they will get a direct answer, and it will not take long. Often the very first thing that pops into their mind is the thing. It may be just the first few words, fleeting pictures, or the tip of the iceberg. Leave room for the shy ones to grow in confidence, but do not let anyone hide out unless they are freaking out.

❧ Summary steps of the exercise

1. Provide a simple teaching (see above) about prophecy and tell them they will be prophesying within ten minutes. Everyone gets nervous.

2. Divide people into groups of three or four and ask for a volunteer in each group to be in the "hot seat." Tell the

volunteer that their job is easy because all they have to do is receive and be the "reporter" of how things may hit them and what is going on inside. They do not have to try to work things up or force something to be relevant.

3. When the leader says, "Ready? Go!" the others have twenty seconds to look at the person in the hot seat and then close their eyes and ask/listen to God. "What nice thing do You have to say about so-and-so?" Any longer and we get into the dreaded "paralysis of analysis."

4. After twenty seconds say, "Ready? Stop!" Then the participants take turns sharing what they thought they heard.

5. When all the participants have shared, the hot-seat person gives feedback. The feedback should be truthful and encouraging. It should follow the advice of Paul to refer to the things that were good. Participants should not comment on the rest.

6. Ask for volunteers to give short testimonies of what happened in their group. Let them speak briefly and to the point. Let faith build. Then do it again, rotating the "hot seat" person.

7. In the end, reinforce the key points. Encourage people to do the exercise together. Challenge people to look for opportunities to give gentle words of encouragement to friends, family, and acquaintances. Remind them to not say, "God told me."

What I Learned
on a Burning Airplane

I want to return to the event that was described at the beginning of this book. The event that kicked off this book's whole thought process—the burning airplane. You'll recall that we landed safely (or there would be no book), deplaned amid foam and fire trucks, and sat 45 minutes waiting for a bus to clear security and come take us to the hangar.

As I sat on the edge of that grassy runway, after I was done shaking and was calm, God seemingly returned to my demanding question I had posed just before the fire interrupted that conversation: "Am I supposed to go into full-time ministry or . . . what?" As I sat there, it seemed that He brought Ephesians 2:10 to my mind, which I'm sure I had once memorized but had since never thought much about. "For we are His workmanship, created in Christ Jesus for good works, which God prepared beforehand so that we would walk in them." And almost immediately, He provided me with a sort of running commentary.

Contained in that one simple verse are all the key truths contained in this book when boiled down to their essence. My hope is that this verse will stick in your memory, and as you think about it, other key truths from the book will bubble up and become yours—yours for life.

In closing, let's unpack this verse together.

I Am God's Workmanship

First, you and I are God's "workmanship." That word carries with it the meaning of "craftsmanship." We are not a cheap, big-box store, assembly-line, pressed-wood bookshelf. IKEA is great, but not for the assembly of humans. That same word is used in Romans 1:20 to depict the very visage of God stamped into the "workmanship" of creation. David spoke of some of what that means.

> For You created my innermost parts; You wove me in my mother's womb. I will give thanks to You, because I am awesomely and wonderfully made; wonderful are Your works, and my soul knows it very well. My frame was not hidden from You when I was made in secret, and skillfully formed in the depths of the earth; Your eyes have seen my formless substance; and in Your book were written all the days that were ordained for me, when as yet there was not one of them. How precious also are Your thoughts for me, God! How vast is the sum of them! Were I to count them, they would outnumber the sand. When I awake, I am still with You.
>
> Psalm 139:13–18

Our body type, soul, personality type, and all else are unique, stamped with the Maker's mark—signed and gifted. Everything about us was carefully chosen by God, perfect both for us and for what He has given us to do in this short life. Everything.

And a key part of that craftsmanship is our inherent, Holy Spirit-supplied *charisma*. As explained in chapters 3 and 4, that *charisma* gift is built into us, part of us from spirit to skin. We see things through its lens, and we are motivated by its influence.

Created in Christ Jesus for Good Works

Second, we are created in Christ to be about doing something—good works. Not only are we carriers of a special *charisma*, but we are also carriers of a special calling supplied and empowered by Jesus—our *diakonia*. Chapters 5 and 6 describe that part of our grace structure. When we each are "about" those things assigned to us, the Body is seen to work like a well-rehearsed orchestra that is conducted by Jesus, the head. That calling for-a-purpose tracks through our whole life. As the verse states, good works, tasks, and jobs. But more than that. At the end of our lives, we will look back and be able to see that which was not always apparent when in the midst of life—each small step of obedient ministry was planned by Jesus to be part of a whole, of a career. And we will see that, as Jesus taught in His parables, faithfulness in small things produced both fruit and promotion. Like Jesus, we are to "be about my Father's business" (Luke 2:49 KJV).

While "works Christianity" gets a bad rap (as well it should, because we are working *because* we are saved, not to get saved), "no works Christianity" should get an equally bad rap.

I was once asked to preach a sermon at a charismatic church I had helped found many years before. Knowing I was moving on soon, I decided to take a chance. I began by exclaiming, "We charismatics, we *love* being a prophetic people of God, casting out demons and going after miracles!" I got a roaring approval. Then I said, "You know, Jesus talked about those things." Everyone smiled and leaned forward to hear what great things Jesus had said about them. I read this passage from Matthew 7.

> "Not everyone who says to Me, 'Lord, Lord,' will enter the kingdom of heaven, but the one who does the will of My Father who is in heaven will enter. Many will say to Me on that day, 'Lord, Lord, did we not prophesy in Your name, and in Your name cast out demons, and in Your name perform many miracles?' And then I will declare to them, 'I never knew you; leave Me, you who practice lawlessness.'"
>
> Matthew 7:21–23

The quiet was tomblike. The normal preacher, who was sitting in the front row, got huge, afraid eyes and slowly shook his head back and forth. I winked and then smiled. He suddenly knew, and he grinned. I told them, "There is a final exam, you know. And Jesus gave us the questions that will be on that exam. Here, in Matthew 25, are those questions contained in the story of the sheep and the goats at the final judgment. Note that both the sheep and the goats were surprised that the things they did, or did not do, were for and with Jesus.

> "Then the righteous will answer Him, 'Lord, when did we see You hungry, and feed You, or thirsty, and give You something to drink? And when did we see You as a stranger, and invite You in, or naked, and clothe You? And when did we see You sick, or in prison, and come to You?' And the King will answer and say to them, 'Truly I say to you, to the extent that you did it for one of the least of these brothers or sisters of Mine, you did it for Me.'"
>
> Matthew 25:37–40

You and I were created to do certain things—good things. And at the end of the age, our knowing about and seeking to work within this *pneumatikos* structure will suddenly be of great importance to us. The test is pass/fail. Understanding that and knowing about the *diakonia* call of Jesus on our lives will help us pass.

That God Prepared Beforehand

Thirdly, there is something special about these good works. They are not just good things—they are *our* good things. They are at the center of the Father's will for our life—prepared for us. They are His *energema* working in our lives. And we are prepared for them. Super good match. Our walk, and a key purpose in this life, is to accomplish certain things. We are to influence and change part of the world—our part. Everything else is more optional, but these works are ours—our calling, job description, and center of focus.

Recall the discussion in chapters 7 and 8 and this verse: "And we know that in all things God works for the good of those who love him, who have been called according to his purpose" (Romans 8:28 NIV). A big part of being called according to His purpose is to understand and purpose ourselves to use our *charisma* and to walk in our assigned *diakonia*—the works prepared for us.

So how do we find these works so that we can walk in them?

I began to ask that question sitting on the runway. The next week, I was sitting in a park on Easter morning, watching a growing gathering of parents. They had come early, ahead of the children, and were placing Easter eggs in and around the picnic area. I could have found them all in five minutes. But the children? It would take longer. The eggs had to be placed just right, visible enough for them to see but hidden enough to create delight in the finding. And I understood something: Good parents know just how to hide Easter eggs *for* the children, not *from* them. *For* not *from*.

That is the nature of the Father's placement of these good works within our lives. Can we find them? Of course! Imagine how maddening and unfair it would be if the works that were prepared for us, and we for them, were hard to find? It is the opposite. Any good father would give his very life to see his children come into all they were created to be. And God is a good Father!

We have to almost try not to find them to actually not find them. In fact, in my experience, discussing this with a large number of people over the years, there seem to be four issues that will keep us from finding them: (1) ignorance that this search is even a thing to focus on; (2) greedy desire and busy eyes for more worldly things; (3) a paralyzing fear of failure stemming from a falsely harsh concept of God; and (4) darkly initiated and humanly accommodated character issues and sin that are not recognized and dealt with.

But I'm convinced of better things concerning you.

For Me to Walk In

Now comes my part—my simple part. How does walking out these works play out in a life?

Walking in these prepared works throughout my life is sort of like watching a child who is doing a dot-to-dot picture. They cannot see the complete drawing that the parent easily distinguishes. But their job, until they do begin to perceive the broader picture, is simply to look for the next dot and connect to that. Wise parents observing their children coax them to go to the next number, even if it seems far from the center of the action.

Like those young children, we need to be okay with the dots that seem far from the action. Sometime later in the dot-to-dot drawing of life, we will look back at the dot line, and we will look ahead and begin to see the whole picture emerge, the pattern and plan. And we will smack our foreheads and say, "He had this planned all along!"

Paul, for example, probably initially thought his time being whisked away to safe Damascus was a waste of time. But those years connected all the dots of the book of Romans, all the wisdom of the Gospel, and made way for much of the New Testament. Moses, too, after growing up in Pharoah's court, might have thought his time herding sheep in the desert was the final failure. But when he was ready, he was called to wisely herd Israelites. The "manna, manna" cries of the people probably sounded strangely like the "baa, baa" of the sheep. David, too, with sheep, and Jesus at twelve wanting to be about His Father's business—maybe everyone is raring to go before their time!

This is where the manifestations of the Spirit in chapters 9 and 10 begin to make sense and become indispensable—God's power tools, perfectly designed to help me as I purpose to walk in the things God has prepared for me.

I'm thankful for the burning airplane. It certainly got my attention, made me listen quietly, and made me smile. Pretty simple in concept. If it was hard to find and do His will, most of us would fail. It is not. Such a great Dad.

It's Yours Now

And you, my friend, who has made it to the end of this book, thank you for taking the time to invest in these understandings and tools.

My prayer is that the key things of the book—the things that God wanted you to get deep down inside—would become yours. Yours. Not borrowed.

May you, my friend, learn to live in connection with the wonderful members of the Trinity. And at the end of your days, may you be able to say, "It was good. These works prepared for me, they were good. And I was well prepared, too."

May you share the Father's smile. See you then. For sure then.

A Few Key Objections or Concerns

Reference Chapter 2

Everyone who has studied and tried to apply the subject of spiritual gifts wishes that Scripture was unambiguous and crystal clear. I certainly do. But it's not. And the results, as described in chapter 1, are diverse and confusing. My goals, as mentioned, are to end up with an approach that is biblical, practical, God-connecting, and transformational. In doing so, I looked carefully at the context in every use of the gifting term we are considering. In the end, I decided to put a lot of weight where Paul seemed to be most pointed and specific: his 1 Corinthians 12 four-part *pneumatikos* analysis, and the places in Scripture where he appeared to explain his *diairesis* analysis using the same key terms as in his 1 Corinthians 12 listing. All other statements seemed to be more comments that could be interpreted many ways, and mostly on the way to some other point (e.g., the lead up to 1 Corinthians 13). Even so, there may be some objections to my conclusions. Here are the most common alternatives as well as my accompanying thoughts.

We Should Combine All Lists

The most common objection is that the various lists of "gifts" in Scripture seem to have overlap in names. Many differences are, perhaps, simply examples of a much larger or even infinite list. In which case, simply combining them into a larger set of examples seems to be the best approach. This idea is expressed by noted scholar Gordon Fee.[1] This argument, however, must deal with Paul's detailed, four-part listing in 1 Corinthians 12, and the most common response is that Paul is simply waxing a bit poetic and emphasizing his point by restating it in different ways.

This argument seems to miss the target on two counts.

First, as mentioned in chapter 9, it seems clear that Paul is talking about four different categories of things of the spirit (not just spiritual gifts) that are related but are very different in kind. They are not comparable, nor are they the same. Referring to these different categories is not like saying we have big and small cans of paint of different colors. It is rather like saying we have paint, painting jobs, painting successes, and different painting tools. That distinction merits a different way of thinking about those verses that has to do with start, cause, and effect. I have a gift, I work in a ministry (within or outside the church walls), and good things happen. And, when needed, manifestations of different types support me and the work. This is very, very different from a simple but awkward combination of everything.

Second, *diairesis* thinking that was discussed in the text would preclude this "just examples" approach. That analysis, even informally, by definition considers the whole of a subject, not a sampling. On close examination of the lists with the four-part structure in mind, I believe you will see that the perceived overlap is not actually an overlap, but simply the same name for a different part of the spirit structure. For example, prophecy is a gift (*charisma*), a prophet is an equipper ministry (*diakonia*) position in a church leadership structure, and speaking a word of prophecy is a (*phanerosis*) manifestation of the Spirit available to all believers. A Prophet is a prophet who prophesies. One who teaches (*charisma*) can also be in a recognized equipper role in the Body as a Pastor or Teacher (*diakonia*). And we all participate in different things at different times that require effort along the lines of any of the seven *charisma* gifts. When a number of Afghan refugees arrived in Nashville in 2022, for example, many in the community dropped everything and gathered to serve and help—gifting in that area or not. A young woman taught us how to help well, even though her *charisma* was not teaching—but serving.

The Word Charisma Is Used in Other Places

A second overall objection is that there are other uses of the word *charisma* in Scripture outside of the Romans 12 listing. Shouldn't they all be taken equally? There are innumerable ways God graces us, and, in some sense, everything we have from Him is a gift—body size and type, family of origin, intelligence, athletic ability, ability to endure hardship, personality type, a "chance" encounter, that pay raise and favor, etc. Paul uses the word *charisma* both generally to define God's grace and specifically to define his *diairesis* analysis.* I wish Paul had strictly limited his use of the word *charisma* like he did *diairesis*—but it is more flexible in usage.

The word "gift" is not understood uniformly and equally in the English language either, and nobody seems to mind. For example, while the word "gift" can be used in a number of ways, you know that by mid-December every child is keenly alert to the use of that word in conjunction with packages under the tree. You would not confuse the uses. Context is key. I think there is a weight of evidence that to classify every use of *charisma* in the New Testament equally is a mistake at odds with Paul's intent. In the context of his *diairesis* analysis, the term has specificity and boundaries. Both Peter and

*Examples include a general grace impartation (see Romans 1:11; 1 Timothy 4:14; 2 Timothy 1:6), salvation (see Romans 5:15), God's general calling and gifting (see Romans 11:29), the ability to live in celibacy (see 1 Corinthians 7:7), the manifestation of different gifts of healings (see 1 Corinthians 12:30), and favor granted to Paul through the prayers of many (see 2 Corinthians 1:11).

Paul make special use of the word *charisma* to describe a singular gift that is given permanently by the Holy Spirit to define an individual's overall body function (e.g., a hand or foot). None of the other uses fit that definition.

Paul Throws Things Together

Finally, a third objection is that, in 1 Corinthians 12:28–31 and 1 Corinthians 14:1, Paul seems to throw together many of the various aspects of spirituality (*pneumatikos*) that he had just laboriously separated in his *diairesis* analysis. The objection is that on the basis of these verses with everything combined, any structure for spiritual gifts may be ill advised. Here are the pertinent verses.

> And God has appointed in the church, first apostles, second prophets, third teachers, then miracles, then gifts of healings, helps, administrations, and various kinds of tongues. All are not apostles, are they? All are not prophets, are they? All are not teachers, are they? All are not workers of miracles, are they? All do not have gifts of healings, do they? All do not speak with tongues, do they? All do not interpret, do they? But earnestly desire the greater gifts [*charisma*]. And yet, I am going to show you a far better way.
>
> 1 Corinthians 12:28–31

In context, Paul has just concluded a detailed discussion about the giving of honor within the Body, and that the parts of the Body with the least visible positions should be deliberately honored in a greater way. It seems that Paul's purpose is to make the point that none of the stew pot of spirituality in chapter 12 matters if it is not seasoned with love in chapter 13. My suspicion is that the use of *charisma* here is similar to the discussion above where he uses that term for the grace of God, and not comparable contextually to the Romans 12 *diairesis* analysis list of seven "functions" in the Body.

In chapter 14, Paul returns to his discussion and refocuses on the specific question the Corinthians asked. He says in 1 Corinthians 14:1 to "pursue love, yet earnestly desire things of the spirit, [*pneumatikos*] but especially that you might prophesy" (author's paraphrase). Again, he returns to use that global term (*pneumatikos*), things of the spirit, to refer to one aspect of that term—the spiritual manifestation of prophecy. Unfortunately, as in 1 Corinthians 12:1, 1 Corinthians 14:1 is most often translated "spiritual gifts" rather than the actual broader term "things of the spirit." Sometimes translations are, in fact, commentaries as well. He reminds them to desire all the things of the spirit, and then highlights, within the context of their question, the superiority of prophecy over uninterpreted tongues in the gathered Church.

Charisma Gift Description Posters

Reference Chapter 4

The Posters

Here are the posters mentioned in chapter 4. The different descriptors originated from many places, and I would err if I tried to recall each one; but there are a few sources that provided important pieces.*

As mentioned in the discussion of the posters, a great way to consider them is to simply go on a "shopping" stroll and see which of the poster descriptions feel most applicable to you. Ask yourself or consider the following:

- What are a couple of things on the poster that jumped out to you?
- What do you love about this gift? What scares you?

*Special thanks to Nancy Arizaga, Bill Gothard, YWAM, The Rock Church, and bits and pieces of 31 different books on the subject.

- Have you and God worked together to use your gift? If so, tell a story about what happened.
- How can others help you grow in this gift?

Go for it. Don't make it hard. No one point is definitive—it is more of a "weight of evidence" approach. You may have an arc that contains some of two adjacent posters. Just look at each poster and get a feel for all of them. Hold them with an open hand and simply whisper somewhere deep within your heart, "Jesus (or Father), which of these things seem most like me?" And listen.

Teaching *didasko*

Acts 18:25; Colossians 1:28

eliminate ignorance/falsehoods
and bring vital, living truth

Basic characteristics:

- You want to make sure statements are true and accurate
- You desire to gain as much knowledge as you can
- You react to people who make unfounded statements
- You check the credentials of one who wants to teach
- You use your mind to check out an argument
- You enjoy spending hours doing research on a subject
- You like to share factual information on a certain topic
- You pay close attention to words and phrases
- You tend to be silent on a matter until you check it out
- You like to study material in a systematic sequence

In church settings, you . . .

- Must validate teaching and sermons
- Procrastinate, need more information, or are slow to make a decision
- Are calm and able to hear God
- Value the Word above experience
- Are loyal to leadership
- May be disorganized
- Stand on conviction but are not judgmental

The mature teacher . . .

1. Is given access by God to deep and applied truth in the Word
2. Uses it to empower and equip
3. Can steward new revelation and can build structures to do so

Exhorting *parakaleo*

Acts 11:23

eliminate confusion
and bring vision and purpose

Basic characteristics:

- You motivate people to become who you see they could be
- You like to give counsel in logical steps of action
- You can usually discern a person's level of spiritual maturity
- You enjoy working out projects to help people grow spiritually
- You sometimes raise expectations of results prematurely
- You dislike teaching that does not give practical direction

- You like to see the facial responses of those you counsel
- You often take "family time" to counsel others
- You enjoy giving examples from others' lives
- You soon give up on those who do not follow your counsel
- You find it hard to follow through on the project you started
- You identify with people where they are to be able to counsel them

In church settings, you . . .

- Are busy, hardworking, diligent, motivational
- May be filled with projects, vision, and relationships
- Can be "too much"
- Are a master communicator and a reconciler of different groups

- Think God is wonderfully extravagant
- Have few relational barriers and a passive leadership style
- Are equipped to counsel, teach, and disciple

The mature exhorter . . .

1. Reveals God to people in a way that influences and brings them to greater potential
2. Brings balance among the other gifts, sees the big picture and road map, and stirs the pot
3. Can move through pain, transforming it and bringing healing
4. Lives/governs by principle more than relationship—solution-oriented

Prophecy *propheteia*

1 Thessalonians 5:20; 1 Timothy 1:18

*eliminate wrong
and bring what is right*

Basic characteristics:

- You see actions as either right or wrong
- You react strongly to people who are not what they appear to be
- You usually detect when something is not what it appears to be
- You can quickly discern a person's character
- You feel a responsibility to correct those who do wrong
- You separate yourself from those who refuse to repent from evil
- You explain what is wrong with an item before you sell it
- You let people know how you feel about important issues
- You enjoy people who are completely honest with you
- You are quick to judge yourself when you fail
- You are willing to do right even if it means suffering alone for it

In church settings, you . . .

- Exhibit black and white, right and wrong thinking
- Express opinions and have passion for excellence
- Are fearless, not intimidated, generous, compulsive
- Are hard on yourself
- Must make sense out of everything
- May feel victimized, transparent, or fearful
- Are drawn to people others reject

The mature prophet . . .

1. Brings God's design and intent
2. Confronts sin and brings grace—speaks the truth into wrong things
3. Builds strong relationships even when "being a prophet"
4. Works with others to bring God's plan to the forefront with insight, seeing into the future, scouting, warning, bringing truth and correction

Serving *diakonia*

1 Corinthians 16:15; 2 Corinthians 9:12

*eliminate physical need
and "get-er-done"*

Basic characteristics:

- You notice the practical needs of others and enjoy meeting them
- You enjoy serving in order to free others for other things
- You are willing to neglect your own work in order to help others
- You sometimes become exhausted in serving others
- You can remember the likes and dislikes of others

- You can usually detect ways to serve before anyone else can
- You will even use your own funds to get a job done quickly
- You do not mind doing jobs yourself
- You don't want public praise but need to feel appreciated
- You find it difficult to say no to those who ask for help
- You like to put "extra touches" on the jobs you do

In church settings, you . . .

- See needs and feel compelled to help meet them
- Find it hard to say no
- Are extremely loyal, can help deep problems
- Extend honor to others, have few enemies but can be dishonored

- Are sentimental and can over-apologize
- Avoid public attention or reputation
- Work hard and can be competitive in sports

The mature server . . .

1. Walks in true humility and knows God well
2. Embraces order and takes personal responsibility
3. Can cause others to want to be holy because of his/her God-pleasing nature
4. Wants the best but sees things honestly—is okay with that
5. Feels God trusts them deeply and gives them unusual authority
6. Engages in healthy service and provides opportunity for others to join in

Mercy *eleeo*

Matthew 5:7; Philippians 2:27

*eliminate pain
and invest in joy*

Basic characteristics:

- You can sense when people have hurt feelings
- You react to those who are insensitive to others' feelings
- You are able to discern genuine love
- You desire deep friendships in which there is mutual commitment
- You seem to attract people who tell you their problems

- You may find it difficult to be firm or decisive with people
- You tend to take up offenses for those you love
- You need quality time to explain how you feel
- You want to remove those who cause hurts to others
- You often wonder why God allows people to suffer

In church settings, you . . .

- Are people focused; feel accepted and safe; hate to confront
- Exhibit the most sensitivity to needs; are often very "prophetic" but with feelings not words
- Access God's heart easily

- Need human intimacy and touch
- Forgive easily, are stubborn (in a nice way), and fight for others
- Are slow to transition or change
- Possess excellent relational and organizational skills

The mature mercy . . .

1. Makes decisions based on values with strong love/mercy
2. Has true empathy and identification with others, leads others to healing and change
3. Not given to emotional extremes, even if strong emotions are felt
4. Emotionally vulnerable but secure and whole
5. Can communicate God's intimacy to others, can draw them to God's grace

Giving *metadidomi*

Ephesians 4:28; 1 Thessalonians 2:8

eliminate resource lack
and invest in high-quality gain

Basic characteristics:

- You are thrifty with money for yourself and your family
- You enjoy investing money in the ministries of others
- You have an ability to make money by wise investments
- You desire to keep your giving secret
- You react negatively to pressure appeals for money
- You like to encourage others to give with your gifts

- You want the ministries you support to be as effective as possible
- You enjoy giving to the needs that others tend to overlook
- You sometimes fear that your gifts will corrupt the receiver
- You desire to give gifts of high quality
- You enjoy knowing that your gifts were specific answers to prayer

In church settings, you . . .

- Exhibit versatility and adaptability, but it is hard to identify these qualities at first
- Are nurturing and deeply committed to family
- Can spot hidden agendas, and it is hard for others to hustle or dupe you

- Receive favor easily
- Relate to a wide range of people in a nonconfrontational way
- Like to give to high-quality causes, not just to the "needy"
- Give more than just money; you provide resources for others

The mature giver . . .

1. Is focused on a life-giving family and a giving culture
2. Has a great practical trust in God based on experience through testing
3. Is not casual about God's absolutes; he or she is principled, holy, not "religious"
4. Gives wisely to help establish works of God
5. Easily accepts responsibility for mistakes

Leading *proistemi*

1 Thessalonians 5:12; 1 Timothy 3:4; 5:17

eliminate group confusion
and invest in vision

Basic characteristics:

- You can visualize the final result of a major undertaking
- You enjoy coordinating the efforts of many to reach a common goal
- You can break down a large task into achievable goals
- You are able to delegate assignments to others
- You often see people as resources that can be used to get a job done

- You are willing to endure reactions to accomplish a task
- You require loyalty in those who are under your supervision
- You remove yourself from petty details to focus on the final goal
- You can encourage your workers and inspire them to action
- You move on to a new challenge once a job is finished

In church settings, you . . .

- Are on time, like to be in charge, and believe the bigger, the better
- Thrive under pressure and even crave it
- Have concerns about loyalty but do not need compliments
- Think, *Don't micromanage me*

- Are a fixer of things and an action taker instead of a blamer
- Are not very spontaneous, like to be asked, and do not see yourself as a volunteer
- Possess diverse skills and can work with imperfect people

The mature leader . . .

1. Can apply pressure with wisdom; is life giving
2. Has high moral integrity; is principled and excellent
3. Engages emotionally and can impart blessing
4. Focuses on the key tasks given by God
5. Draws balance from other gifts; seeks wise counsel
6. Is given authority and government in the Kingdom

God's Truth and Warnings about Gifting

Reference Chapter 4

God, through Peter, Paul, and Mary's son, Jesus, expresses a few nonnegotiables concerning *charisma* gifts. We would do well to heed these nonnegotiables and build them into our lives and the life of the church, organization, or structure in which we operate. I have decided to place them in an appendix not because they are not important, but because they are important enough to consider separately and not as a part of a larger chapter.

My Gift Is Used for God's Glory

A gift is used to glorify God (see 1 Peter 4:11). Like the issue of gift ownership (we are stewards, as Key 5 in chapter 3 states), the surest way to disfigure a gifting is to employ it in self-promotion. It then becomes a caricature of God's intent. When gifts (and manifestations) of the Spirit are used, even partially, for showmanship or to build an audience, people become more connected to the gifted one and less to God. People love heroes who are heroic. God loves heroes who wash feet.

A big problem with misusing gifts, which seems rampant in some denominations, is twofold. First, we must clearly understand that being a follower of Jesus is very different from being a follower of a "follower" of Jesus. Followers of self-proclaimed followers of Jesus have been repeatedly lured into diabolical, anti-Jesus missions, each one in clear violation of Jesus' direct teaching on honor, service, greed, humility, forgiveness, and much more.

Jesus Himself warned of this. "An hour is coming for everyone who kills you to think that he is offering a service to God" (John 16:2). And, "See to it that you are not misled; for many will come in My name, saying, 'I am He,'" (Luke 21:8).

If "followers of followers" would have been simply followers of Jesus' teachings over the last two thousand years, there would have been no black eyes for "Christianity." No Inquisition, no Crusades, no pogroms, no Holocaust, no religious wars, no Catholic or Protestant religious persecution, no enslavement of Africans or abuse of Native Americans, and no stealing of tribal gold, diamonds, oil, or other resources. And there would be no strange mixing of nationalism with simple Jesus-following . . . on both the right and the left. There would be no pressure to abandon godly, just causes simply because some who also support them are not like us up and down the line.

Simple followers and their bands of cofollowers would have drastically changed the whole course of history and led the world along a different path—the path of peace, and not as the world brings it (see John 14:27). If I want to be a leader in bringing peace, I must be a simple follower.

Second, as in Corinth, everyone tried to be "spiritual," and the measure of that spirituality was the showy public use of manifestations. Their effectiveness is diminished to that of a public show. Jesus often said about His miracles and signs, "Tell no one." He did not say, "Tell everyone." As we look to some television preachers and some forms of Christianity, we clearly see this particular issue being played out.

But, as the next key explains, when we use what has been given (gifts and manifestations) to quietly glorify God and to serve in the "foot washing" position, the aroma or flavor of the gifting is wonderful, and people are attracted to us. They quickly realize it is God in us to which they are attracted (see 2 Corinthians 2:15). God has no grandchildren. Woe to the ones who step in between God and His children by standing in the limelight. Better to be like Mother Teresa.

My Gift Is Used to Serve Others

Not only are we not to claim ownership or obtain glory from the gifts, but they are to be used in serving others. Even the speaking gifts are to be used to serve. This gift use is a safety factor. In the world, we are encouraged to use our gifting and talent to become successful in careers and become wealthy, important, recognized, and dominant. This is not the way of Christ, and not the way of the use of His gifts. The Head of the Body clearly says that "the greatest of you shall be your servant" (Matthew 23:11) and to "seek first His kingdom and His righteousness, and all these things will be provided to you" (Matthew 6:33).

Together We Create a Culture of Honor

I was part of a church in which "prophets" would come to town and obtain a speaking engagement at the church. I observed a dynamic that was almost always harmful. These men and women would demonstrate undeniable, powerful, and honest manifestations of God. Everyone would be impressed. Great, huh? Not at all. The problem with such highly gifted ones standing in front and demonstrating, without humble impartation and teaching of others, was that most everyone in the audience thought two things: "They are *amazing!*" and "I could *never* do that. So I won't." Instead of those who were greatly gifted using their maturity to equip others, they used it to impress, gain a following, and earn a living—and leave.

This scenario is not God's best, nor is it His intent.

After Paul lays out both the structure of the package and the list of the manifestations in 1 Corinthians 12, he turns to the attitude issues in the Corinthian church that probably helped lead to the show-off culture. And in so doing, he turns from manifestations (*phanerosis*) to gifts (*charisma*) within the Body. In summary, he says you may feel as though you and your role are unimportant, or that you and your role are very important. Neither belief is true. He then lays out the true and right understanding of how the Church is to show honor:

> But now God has arranged the parts, each one of them in the body, just as He desired. . . . On the contrary, it is much truer that the parts of the body which seem to be weaker are necessary; and those parts of the body which we consider less honorable, on these we bestow greater honor, and our less presentable parts become much more presentable, whereas our more presentable parts have no need of it. But God has so composed the body, giving more abundant honor to that part which lacked, so that there may be no division in the body, but that the parts may have the same care for one another.
>
> 1 Corinthians 12:18, 22–25

The whole point of this discussion on honor is that comparison among Body members in terms of gifting and, thus, importance, is false. In his second letter to the Corinthians, to ensure they get this point, he states, "When they measure themselves by themselves and compare themselves with themselves, they have no understanding" (2 Corinthians 10:12). Want to compete? As Paul says, just after his gift listing in Romans, "Outdo one another in showing honor" (Romans 12:10 ESV). Same care. Differing honor. When a church begins to focus on honor, the foot-washing kind, on the serving gifts (because the healthy speaking gifts rarely need such deliberate honor-giving—it comes with the gifting), the result is amazing unity, flowing grace, and a sense of awe. And the Body grows—not just the numbers who attend on Sunday.

Do I Lose My Gifting through Disobedience?

What if we are disobedient to that tug of God? Will we change or lose our gifting? I don't think so. In my experience, we just go around the mountain again, arriving back at the place of calling. Paul says, "The gifts and the calling of God are irrevocable [without repentance]" (Romans 11:29). In context, he was referring to God's plan for the Jews, but I have found it to be applicable generally.

Paul is simply saying that you cannot stop being you. Your gift and calling are yours for life. Whether you excel in them or ignore them, they are still yours. And God will not stop being Himself through you. It is not "use it or lose it." Gifts are part of who we are, part of our spiritual genetics, and are unchanging in type. Our primary color will always remain the same on earth. The works God has for us to do are our responsibility.

Detailed Manifestations Descriptions

Reference Chapter 9

This Appendix contains descriptions of the nine manifestations of the Spirit listed in 1 Corinthians 12:7–11. Like Appendix B (the *charisma* gift posters), these descriptions are an amalgamation of over 45 years of input and experience across a broad spectrum of the Church and are derived from ideas from over thirty books and other sources. In that time, I have been a keen student of various leaders, congregations, and sources. I took notes on the various expressions and practices, comparing them to Scripture, observing their fruit, and throwing out obvious nonsense. I'm sure improvements can still be made in definitions and applications, and the manifestations are far more flexible than any of us know.

I encourage you to read them in that light, look at the Scripture verses given, and make your own decision to pursue these things of the spirit for the purpose of using them to assist in the work of God through you: your Holy Spirit *charisma* gifting, working through your Jesus-led *diakonia* ministry, steered and resourced by the *energema* of your loving Father.

Such fun!

Various Kinds of Tongues

Acts 2:4; 10:46; 19:6

There are various kinds of tongues (men, angels, demonic), and one who speaks in a tongue may sometimes slip into several different-sounding tongues, perhaps to pray in a different way or with a different focus.

You can see from the description of tongues in chapters 9 and 10 that there are both many good reasons *to* speak in tongues and some guidance given on *when* and *where* to speak in tongues. The reasons and scriptural encouragement given to speak in tongues should be sufficient to dispel hesitancy or distaste for tongues that we may have previously acquired.

Tongues seem to come with two basic purposes, both in Scripture and in present experience: One purpose is to communicate, and the other is to pray or worship privately. When we do so privately, we pray from within our spirit, and the prayer should then be complete—true and without mixture.

Some feel the verse in Romans 8:26 (about the Holy Spirit helping us to pray with "groanings too deep for words") refers to tongues. Others feel that Ephesians 6:18 and Jude 1:20 (about praying in/ with the Spirit/spirit) also refer to praying in tongues. We must be careful not to set limits beyond clear scriptural truth. It seems to me that tongues is one kind of praying in the spirit, but a person can pray in English led by the Spirit and have it be just as "in the spirit."

The Interpretation of Tongues

Acts 2:8; 10:46

The interpretation of tongues is the supernatural giving of the "sense" or "meaning" of a spoken tongue, yours or another's. It is to be distinguished from "translation," which is a word-for-word rendering. An interpretation faithfully gives the equivalent meaning of what was said but in the interpreter's own words. The interpretation may come to the speaker in a number of ways, such as an inner vision, a few words, a picture, seeing writing, a general sense, etc. Thus, the interpretation often comes to the one given the manifestation as a complete thought, as a certain "knowing," or even as a few words with the inner assurance that once he or she starts to speak, the rest will begin to flow. It's sort of like seeing the end of a string but knowing the rest of the string will come if you pull on the end.

The purpose of this manifestation is generally to render the manifestation of tongues intelligible to the hearer. There are not many examples of it in Scripture, but there is sufficient teaching in 1 Corinthians 12–14 on it. From experience in the Church, there seems to be several forms this manifestation may take, including occurrence of the ability to hear someone speaking in your own tongue (there is some difference of opinion about just how the manifestation took place on the day of Pentecost: Was the miracle in the speaking or in the hearing?), the supernatural occurrence of the ability to understand a foreign tongue known to the speaker but not to you, and the occurrence of the ability to interpret an unknown language manifestation of tongues.

It is clear from Scripture that not all tongues need interpretation. Those tongues that are intended for communication need an interpretation (see 1 Corinthians 14:5, 13, 28):

- "Now I wish that you all spoke in tongues, but rather that you would prophesy; and greater is the one who prophesies than the one who speaks in tongues, unless he interprets, so that the church may receive edification" (1 Corinthians 14:5).
- "Therefore, one who speaks in a tongue is to pray that he may interpret" (1 Corinthians 14:13).
- "If anyone speaks in a tongue, it must be by two or at the most three, and each one in turn, and one is to interpret;

but if there is no interpreter, he is to keep silent in church; and have him speak to himself and to God" (1 Corinthians 14:27–28).

- "For this reason the one who speaks in a tongue should pray that they may interpret what they say" (1 Corinthians 14:13 NIV).

Sometimes, in your private prayer time when you are praying in tongues, God may begin to show you how the manifestation of interpretation of tongues can work within and through you. You can practice it using your own manifestation of tongues while in personal intercession.

Prophecy

Acts 7:2; 11:28; 13:2; 19:6; 21:4, 11

The spiritual manifestation of prophecy is speaking the thoughts or words of God to others. It is almost never a word-for-word mimicking where the speaker is sort of a robotic mouthpiece. It is normally the speaker giving the sense, key phrase, or specific single word they heard, saw, or sensed within themselves. It sometimes may be explained as "thought rhyming" the sense of what God is saying. If the speaker goes beyond what he hears or senses, those around can normally tell the difference. We have trouble sounding like God when we don't have God's words.

The key to understanding this mixture is to grasp Paul's phrase in 1 Corinthians 13:9, which says, "We prophesy in part." And thus, Paul gives us a warning not to "utterly reject prophecies, but examine everything; hold firmly to that which is good" (1 Thessalonians 5:20–21). There are many examples in Scripture: revelation of a ministry (see 1 Timothy 1:18), speaking spontaneously when filled with the Holy Spirit (see Acts 19:6), or Barnabas first arriving at Antioch (see Acts 11:23).

Paul says, "The one who prophesies speaks to people for edification, exhortation, and consolation" (1 Corinthians 14:3). Suffice to say here that the one who prophesies does so to edify (build up) the hearer(s).

The following statement may run counter to some thinking that the prophet only speaks hell, fire, and damnation. Prophecy is most often strong truth that brings great encouragement. It reflects the heart of God, who most often speaks love to His children. It can sometimes be compared to a trick-shot artist. God would like to speak directly to someone but, for some reason, they cannot hear what He has to say. So He "bounces" His word off another, who can hear and faithfully relate what God is saying. It can also convict and teach believers as well as unbelievers.

The Word of Knowledge

Acts 5:3; 8:26; 9:10; 10:5; 16:6–7, 9; 18:9; 20:23; 23:11; 27:10, 23

The supernatural occurrence of the ability to know a fact or other specific information about a person, situation, or thing by revelation of the Holy Spirit apart from, but not necessarily contrary to, our natural senses or sources of information.

The goal of the word of knowledge is often to produce conviction, action, or change in a situation or person. Jesus used a word of knowledge with the woman at the well to bring her and the town to salvation (see John 4:17). Paul was warned of the impending shipwreck (see Acts 27:10, 23) and used that knowledge to influence the sailors and to strengthen himself. Agabus used it to bring assistance to Jerusalem during a famine (see Acts 11:28).

Words of knowledge can come through a number of channels and methods, including an internal impression, sense, or feeling, a picture, a sensation in the body, a dream, a vision, an audible voice, a quickening of a Scripture passage, etc. A word of knowledge should always be applied sensitively and properly with love as the motive and humility as the means. Pray for wisdom to interpret and apply the revelation, and ask for help from those in authority. Check your motive about drawing attention to yourself. Give it discreetly.

The Distinguishing of Spirits

Acts 8:21; 13:9–11; 16:16; 17:16; 19:16–17; 22:21

The distinguishing of spirits is the occurrence of the ability to perceptively distinguish among spiritual sources or provide judicial estimation on the source. It often includes the intent of spirits: human, demonic, angelic, or divine—to be able to tell spiritual motivation or source. Jesus, for example, distinguished sources when Satan spoke through Peter (see Matthew 16:23) or when the sons of Zebedee wanted to call fire down on Samaritan cities (see Luke 9:54). It can include the occurrence of the ability to discern the line between human and divine action and motivation, to tell kinds of demonic spirits (see Mark 9:29), to distinguish character (see John 1:47), or to see the motivation behind words or actions (see Philippians 1:15–17).

The manifestation is given to provide warning or deliverance, or to reveal and expose Satan's plans or servants. It is given to expose error or the flesh, to expose false motivation, to head off evil intent, and more. For example, it was needed but not evident in Galatia (see Galatians 1:6–9) and is necessary for the Lord's bondservants (see 2 Timothy 2:24–26).

All revelation must be tested and sensitively applied to the situation, even more so with this manifestation. Watch over yourself that you don't use quick, thoughtless words or actions. Do not become offended at false spirits or the flesh. Correct and move with gentleness. The goal is love and restoration, *not* harsh exposure. Although sometimes, especially when dealing with wanton rebellion, decisive actions are necessary. Pray for wisdom. Cultivate this gift by growing in maturity through exercising spiritual senses and spiritually interpreting what the physical senses indicate (see Hebrews 5:14).

The Word of Wisdom

Acts 3:24; 6:10; 9:15; 10:15; 13:46; 14:22; 15:28; 17:22; 21:23; 22:21; 23:6

A word of wisdom is a supernatural occurrence of the ability to know or understand the ways and/or plans of God for a specific situation. Words of wisdom are to be spoken out to articulate the specific wisdom of God in the situation. It is "God's view" (which is "the" view) on a certain subject or in a certain situation.

Jesus exhibited this manifestation when He confounded His opponents (see Matthew 22:22). The Jerusalem elders and apostles relied on it when they sought how to answer the Antioch church about circumcision (see Acts 15:28). A word of wisdom often works after or with a word of knowledge, prophecy, or other revelation in that it is then the revelation on the decision about what to do with the revelatory word.

A word of wisdom can flow individually or as part of a group decision-making process. The word of wisdom is always tied to the intent of Scripture and often in application of specific principles or verses. It is often used by God to solve tough problems, and it produces a sense of rightness, unity, or unanimity. People jointly feel a bit of awe at what has transpired.

Growing in the use of this gift is tied with growing our character and in knowing the character and ways of God. When we are steeped in His ways, hearing and discerning His wisdom seems to come much easier.

Gifts of Healings

Acts 3:6; 5:16; 9:18, 34; 14:10; 19:11; 28:8–9

The supernatural occurrence of the ability, through some action, word, or prayer, to bring about or serve as a conduit for healing in a specific situation or situations. It often involves several manifestations at the same time. More accurately, it extends the other manifestations into the realm of actually bringing about a change in the physical world. The healing is the gift, not the person God uses. Examples are throughout the gospels and the book of Acts.

There is actually a double plural "gifts" of "healings." This implies (and history and observation support this thought) that there are different modes of operation for healing as well as different types of healing. Healing may be both physical and emotional, it may be instantaneous or gradual (see John 4:52), or it may work much more slowly as it initiates and speeds up the natural process. It may require concerted and prolonged or repeated prayer (sometimes called "soaking" prayer). It may come from laying on hands, a simple prayer, speaking a word, some physical (even symbolic) action, a point of contact, singing and worship, or any number of other ways. An individual may operate in a unique or even unusual way to employ the gift of healings. The manifestation may be distinguished from praying for healing generally or from calling for the elders to lay on hands (see James 5).

This is not "name it and claim it" faith healing but is initiated by God for a certain person in a specific instance. Or it is initiated by God in support of a ministry (such as preaching the Gospel) where it often occurs both to heal and to witness to the Word being preached (see Hebrews 2:4).

I believe God wants to heal much more than we see healing, but He often finds us unable to believe, receive, or initiate effectively the word He gives. He finds us weak spiritually and shrinking back from either stepping out or persevering in prayer when we don't see immediate results. In Mark 6 and Matthew 13, it is said that Jesus could not perform many miracles in His hometown, and He marveled at their unbelief. This need to step out in faith must be distinguished from, and balanced against, the natural emotional desire to see someone who is suffering healed and the soul-inspired prayer that often follows.

The Effecting of Miracles

Acts 5:12; 6:8; 8:6; 9:40; 14:3; 16:26; 19:11; 20:10; 28:6

The literal translation of this phrase is "the energizings of powers." The words are *energema*, and *dunamis*, the Greek word for power. This is God working through a person to interrupt the natural world by His power so that He can bring about His intended action and purpose. A miracle occurs when the supernatural world invades the physical world to make a change that is apart from natural laws: changing water into wine, multiplying fish and loaves, walking on water, calming storms. These words are also a double plural, carrying the same implication as "gifts of healings." There can be many modes of operation and many types of miracles.

It might be said that healing is a subset of this manifestation. Some have gone so far as to say that the healing manifestation is gradual while this manifestation is always instantaneous, or that this manifestation works a miracle while the faith manifestation receives a miracle already worked.

A miracle, like most manifestations, occurs when the will of God intersects the faithful obedience of man. Miracles can occur in many ways similar to healing. God often requires some symbolic or related act of obedience to bring about the miracle, such as Moses' arms being held up to bring about victory, filling water jugs before they became wine, etc. Lack of faith can (but not always will) interrupt or limit a miracle even though God is willing to bring it about. An example of this is when Peter sank in the water after stepping from the boat at the command of Jesus.

Faith

Acts 4:19, 29; 7:56; 14:9

The definition of faith is the supernatural occurrence of the ability to believe for a specific thing, or in a specific situation, beyond one's normal or usual ability, or faith because of the specific revelation of God (as in, "I know this sounds a bit strange, but I am pretty certain God told me that . . ."). It is an inner knowing about a certain situation, not necessarily so much factually (more of a word of knowledge) but a knowing that it will turn out okay, that something will surely happen, or that God will absolutely intervene. It is a surge of confidence or irresistible certainty that God will act in a certain way. This is often accompanied by authority to pray or speak in such a way as to affect this intervention of God.

Jesus spoke the certainty of Lazarus' resurrection (see John 11:42), and Peter and Paul saw faith residing in a person and healed them (see Acts 3:7; Acts 14:9). The manifestation rarely works without one of the others with it. It is both a revelation of fact (a word of knowledge) and the faith to know with certainty the outcome intended by God. Thus, in a way, faith extends the other manifestations into the realm of causation, causing something to come about through belief.

The manifestation of faith is different from general faith for salvation or for general protection, provision, etc., which relies more on the character of God and overall promises. This manifestation is revealed faith that is targeted at a specific objective either for an individual or for a situation. It can also seem to manifest as a continuing occurrence of the ability, or sustained belief, to function in a certain power ministry day in and day out. For example, someone who prays for healing and miracles often could have the manifestation of faith. This manifestation is the "I know that I know that I know" faith.

Notes

Chapter 1 We Have a Problem

1. Larry Gilbert, "How Many Spiritual Gifts Are There?," ChurchGrowth.org, accessed February 17, 2023, https://churchgrowth.org/how-many-spiritual-gifts-are-there/.

2. Wayne Grudem, *Are Miraculous Gifts for Today?: Four Views* (Grand Rapids: Zondervan, 1996).

3. Sam Storms, *The Beginner's Guide to Spiritual Gifts* (Minneapolis: Bethany House, 2012); Sam Storms, *Practicing the Power: Welcoming the Gifts of the Holy Spirit in Your Life* (Grand Rapids: Zondervan, 2017).

4. Harvey Floyd, *Is the Holy Spirit for Me?* (Nashville: 20th Century Christian, 1981); Tim Woodruff, *A Spirit for the Rest of Us* (Abilene: Leafwod, 2009); Leonard Allen, *Poured Out: The Spirit of God Empowering the Mission of God* (Abilene: Abilene Christian University Press, 2018).

5. C. Peter Wagner, *Your Spiritual Gifts Can Help Your Church Grow* (Minneapolis: Chosen, 2012); Rick Yohn, *Discover Your Spiritual Gift and Use It* (Carol Stream, IL: Tyndale House, 1974); Robert Heidler, *Experiencing the Spirit: Developing a Living Relationship with the Holy Spirit* (Minneapolis: Chosen, 1998); Darren Tyler, *The Power of the Seven: Discover, Develop, and Deliver the World-Shifting Life Gifts of Romans 12* (self-pub., 2020).

6. S. D. Choi, *The Correlation of Personality Factors with Spiritual Gifts Clusters* (PhD diss., Andrews University, 1993).

7. K. J. Stone, *Relationships between Personality and Spiritual Gifts* (PhD diss., George Fox University, 1991).

8. Jason Hawthorne, "Part I: Spiritual Gift / Personality Type Comparisons," January 22, 2006, https://spiritualgiftpersonalitytypecomparisons.wordpress.com/part-i-spiritual-gift-personality-type-comparisons/; Aurelian, "Spiritual Gifts Research," February 17, 2007, http://spiritualgiftsresearch.blogspot.com/2007/02/can-gifts-and-personality-be.html.

9. Rick Warren, "Your SHAPE Shows Your Purpose," PastorRick.com, April 13, 2021, https://pastorrick.com/your-shape-shows-your-purpose/; Network was developed by Bruce Bugbee, and resources can be found at https://www.brucebugbee.com/other-resources; Dr. Mels Carbonell, UniquelyYou.org.

Chapter 2 Paul's Analysis of Spiritual Things

1. James A. Philip, "Platonic Diairesis," *Proceedings of the American Philological Association* 97 (1966): 335–358.
2. *Thayer's Greek-English Lexicon of the New Testament* (1995), s.v. "διαίρεσις."
3. F. F. Bruce, *Paul: Apostle of the Heart Set Free* (Grand Rapids: Eerdman's, 1977); Paul Barnett, *Paul, Missionary of Jesus* (Grand Rapids: Eerdman's, 2008); Orville Boyd Jenkins, "When Paul Studied with Gamaliel," Practical Approaches to Life and Reality, accessed February 17, 2023, http://orvillejenkins.com/theology/paulrabbiage.html.

Chapter 3 The Spirit and Charisma Gifts

1. *Thayer's*, s.v. "πρᾶξις."
2. Bible Hub, s.v. "4291.proistemi," https://biblehub.com/greek/4291.htm.

Chapter 5 Jesus and Ministry

1. Todd M. Johnson and Gina A. Zurlo, eds., *World Christian Encyclopedia Online* (Boston: Brill, 2019), https://referenceworks.brillonline.com/browse/world-christian-encyclopedia-online.
2. Greg L. Hawkins and Cally Parkinson, *Move: What 1,000 Churches Reveal about Spiritual Growth* (Grand Rapids: Zondervan, 2016).

Chapter 6 Finding My Ministry

1. Frederick Buechner, *Wishful Thinking: A Seeker's ABC* (San Francisco: HarperOne, 1993), 119.

Chapter 7 The Father and Life

1. Quoted in Watchman Nee, *The Normal Christian Life* (Carol Stream, IL: Tyndale, 1977), 135–137.

Chapter 8 The Father's Smile

1. Andy Reese and Jennifer Barnett, *Freedom Tools: For Overcoming Life's Tough Problems*, rev. and upd. ed. (Minneapolis: Chosen, 2015), 48.
2. Will Ashton, "The Spider-Man Scene That Took Tobey Maguire 156 Takes," Cinema Blend, January 11, 2022, https://www.cinemablend.com/news/2475260/the-spider-man-scene-that-took-tobey-maguire-156-takes.

Chapter 9 The Holy Spirit and Manifestations

1. Bible Hub, s.v. "5316.phainó," https://biblehub.com/greek/5316.htm; s.v. "5319.phaneroó," https://biblehub.com/greek/5319.htm.
2. N. T. Wright, "#29 The Charismatic Gifts of the Spirit," January 24, 2020, in *Ask NT Wright Anything* podcast, https://askntwrightanything.podbean.com/e/29-the-charismatic-gifts-of-the-spirit/.
3. Francis MacNutt, "The Mystery: Why Some Are Healed and Others Are Not," *Healing Line*, November/December 1991, https://www.christianhealingmin.org/index.php/hl-issue-1991-5/333-magazine/1991-1995/hl-articles-1991-5/1400-the-mystery-why-some-are-healed-others-are-not.
4. See Reese and Barnett, *Freedom Tools*.

5. Owen Bourgaize, "D. L Moody Was Once Asked Why He Urged Christians," Sermon Central, June 3, 2001, https://www.sermoncentral.com/sermon-illustrations/2970/d-l-moody-was-once-asked-why-he-urged-christians-by-owen-bourgaize.

Chapter 10 Tongues and Prophecy

1. Mel Tari with Cliff Dudley, *Like a Mighty Wind* (Lake Mary, FL: Creation House, 1971).

2. Eddie L. Hyatt, *2000 Years of Charismatic Christianity: A 21st Century Look at Church History from a Pentecostal/Charismatic Perspective* (Lake Mary, FL: Charisma House, 2002).

3. Quoted in Hyatt, *2000 Years of Charismatic Christianity*, 16.

4. "Global Christianity—A Report on the Size and Distribution of the World's Christian Population," Pew Research Center, December 19, 2011, https://www.pewresearch.org/religion/2011/12/19/global-christianity-exec/.

5. Among many references, Constance Holden, "Tongues in the Mind," *Science Now* 2006, no. 336 (November 2, 2006), 3; see also Lightworkers, "Medical Study Proves Validity of Speaking in Tongues," Voices, *The Christian Post*, August 2, 2019, https://www.christianpost.com/voices/medical-study-proves-validity-speaking-in-tongues.html; and www.andrewnewberg.com.

6. Charles J. Limb and Allen R. Braun, "Neural Substrates of Spontaneous Musical Performance: An fMRI Study of Jazz Improvisation," *PLoS ONE* 3, no. 2 (February 27, 2008), https://doi.org/10.1371/journal.pone.0001679.

7. Leslie Francis and Mandy Robbins, "Personality and Glossolalia: A Study Among Male Evangelical Clergy," abstract, *Pastoral Psychology* 51, no. 5 (May 2003), 391–396, https://link.springer.com/article/10.1023/A:1023618715407.

8. Felicitas D. Goodman, *Speaking in Tongues: A Cross-Cultural Study of Glossolalia* (Eugene, OR: Wipf and Stock, 2008).

9. John P. Kildahl, "Psychological Observations," in *The Charismatic Movement*, ed. Michael P. Hamilton (Grand Rapids: Eerdmans, 1975), 142.

10. Nicholas P. Spanos, et al., "Glossolalia As Learned Behavior: An Experimental Demonstration," *Journal of Abnormal Psychology* 95, no. 1 (1986), 21–23.

11. Sara Forsberg, "What Languages Sound Like to Foreigners," YouTube.com, March 3, 2014, https://youtu.be/ybcvlxivscw.

Appendix A

1. Gordon D. Fee, *God's Empowering Presence: The Holy Spirit in the Letters of Paul* (Grand Rapids: Baker Academic, 2011).

Andy Reese is a thankful follower of God, a lucky husband, a proud father and grandfather, an engineer, a writer, and a serial idea entrepreneur.

Professionally, he is a well-known thought leader in rainwater management and green sustainable design, having coauthored *Municipal Stormwater Management* (Lewis Publishers, 2003). He taught at Vanderbilt and Lipscomb Universities and has given many national and international keynote addresses. He is the coauthor of *Freedom Tools* (Chosen Books, 2015) and helps lead a multinational, nonprofit ministry (Freedom Prayer—www.freedomprayer.org) that seeks to help bring freedom and spiritual vitality to believers. He is the author of several other books and is the developer of "Magi," a presentation of the science, geography, history, and culture explaining the authenticity of the Star of Bethlehem story. This presentation has over 100,000 YouTube views.